Clara Litabeark

W. K. W.

OLD SHRINES AND IVY

OLD SHRINES
AND IVY

BY

WILLIAM WINTER

" I do love these ancient ruins:
We never tread upon them but we set
Our foot upon some reverend history.
. . . But all things have their end"
THE DUCHESS OF MALFI

NEW YORK
MACMILLAN AND COMPANY
AND LONDON
1894

Norwood Press:
J. S. Cushing & Co. — Berwick & Smith.
Boston, Mass., U.S.A.

TO

George William Curtis

WITH HONOUR FOR A NOBLE MIND

AND A BEAUTIFUL LIFE

AND WITH AFFECTIONATE MEMORIES

OF MUCH KINDNESS

DURING MORE THAN THIRTY YEARS OF

UNCLOUDED FRIENDSHIP

I DEDICATE THIS BOOK

"Ibimus, ibimus,
Utcunque præcedes, supremum
Carpere iter comites parati"

PREFACE.

THE shrines upon which these offerings of homage are laid are shrines of history and shrines of literature. It has been the author's design, alike in description and commentary, and whether depicting scenes of travel or celebrating achievements of genius, to carry through his books the thread of Shakespearean interest. The study of Shakespeare is the study of life. There can be no broader or higher subject. In these sketches and essays, accordingly, the reader is desired not only to ramble in various parts of England, Scotland, and France, but especially to linger for a while in lovely Warwickshire, and to meditate upon some of the works of that divine poet with whose story and whose spirit that region is hal-

7

lowed. *Historical facts that are recounted,
in the course of these papers, respecting
Shakespeare pieces and a few others, are
not new to the dramatic scholar; but even
to him a summary of knowledge, combined
with definite thought, as to those writings,
may prove not unwelcome.*

*Most of the essays on the plays were writ-
ten at the suggestion of my old friend
Augustin Daly, and were privately printed,
by way of introduction to stage-versions of
those plays, edited by him. A thread of
theatrical history therefore appears in those
essays, entwined with disquisition on the
beauties of some of the most cherished treasures of our language. The paper commemorative of Longfellow was written in the
New York Tribune at the time of his death.*

W. W.

MAY. 1892.

CONTENTS.

I. SHRINES OF HISTORY.

9

II. SHRINES OF LITERATURE.

I

SHRINES OF HISTORY

OLD SHRINES AND IVY.

I.

STORIED SOUTHAMPTON.

EARLY in the morning of a brilliant July day the Scilly islands came into view, a little to the south of our course, and we could see the great waves breaking into flying masses and long wreaths of silver foam, on their grim shores and in their rock-bound chasms. Yet a little while and the steep cliffs of Cornwall glimmered into the prospect, and then came the double towers of the Lizard Light, and we knew that our voyage was accomplished. The rest of the way is the familiar panorama of the channel coast — lonely Eddystone, keeping its sentinel watch in solitude and danger ; the green pasture lands of Devon ; the crags of Portland, gray and emerald and gold, shining, changing, and fading in silver mist ; the shelving fringes of the Solent ; the sandy coves and green hills of the beautiful Isle of Wight; and placid Southampton Water with its little light-houses and its crescent town, vital with the incessant enterprise of the present and rich with splendid associations of the past. The gloaming had begun to die into night when we landed, and in the sleepy stillness of the vacant streets and of the quiet inn we were soon conscious of that feeling of peace and comfort which is the first sensation of the old traveller who comes again into England. It is the sensation — after long wandering and much vicissitude — of being at home and at rest; and you seldom, or never, find it elsewhere.

If the old city of Southampton were not, to the majority of ramblers, merely a port of entry and departure, if the traveller were constrained to seek it as a goal instead of treating it as a thoroughfare, its uncommon physical beauty and its exceptional anti-quarian interest would be more fitly appre-ciated and more highly prized than they appear to be at present. Objects that are viewed as incidental are seldom compre-hended as important. Traffic, with its attendant bustle, imparts to Southampton shores an air of turbulence and common-ness. The popular spirit of our age, notwithstanding there is a newly awakened feeling of reverence actively at work, makes no account of picturesque accessories and does nothing either to create or to perpetuate them. In Southampton, for example, just as in ancient Warwick, a tramcar jangles through the grim arch of a gray stone gate of the Middle Ages; and this way the Present makes its comment on the Past. Yet the Present and the Past are inseparably associated, — the one being the consequence and inheritor of the other, — and in no way better can the student of social development pursue his study than in rambling through the streets and among the structures that to-day has built amid the ruins and the relics of yesterday. A walk in breezy Southampton was full of instruction. There was a great and merry multitude upon the lovely green Common, when first I saw it, a band was playing in its pavilion, and birds were circling and twittering around the tree-tops in the light of the evening sun; but as I stood there and watched the happy throng and listened to the martial music the scene seemed suddenly to change, and I beheld the armoured cohorts of Henry V., and heard the trumpets bray, and saw the gallant king, upon his mail-clad charger, riding downward to the sea, for Agincourt and the laurel of everlasting fame.

Many days might be pleasantly spent in Southampton and its storied neighbourhood. You are at the mouth of the Itchen — the river of Izaak Walton, who lived and died at venerable Winchester, only a few miles away. Netley Abbey is close by. On every side, indeed, there is something to stimulate the fancy and to awaken remembrance of historic lore. King John's house is extant, in Blue Anchor lane. King John's charter may be seen in the Audit House. The Bridewell Gate still stands, that was built by Henry VIII., and in Bugle street is the Spanish prison that was used in the time of Queen Anne. At the foot of the High street stood King Canute's palace; and upon the neighbouring beach the monarch spoke his vain command to stay the advancing waves and made his memorable submission to the Power that is greater than kings. In St. Michael's square they show you an ancient red-tiled house, made of timber and brick, in which Anne Boleyn once lived, with her royal lord Henry VIII., and which bears her name to this day. It is a two-story building, surmounted with four large gables, the front curiously diversified with a crescent pent and with four great diamond-latticed casements ; and gazing upon it I could not fail to conjure up a vision of that dark-eyed, golden-haired beauty whose fascination played so large a part in shaping the religious and political destiny of England. There she may have stood, in the gloaming, and looked forth upon the grim and gloomy Norman church that still frowns upon the lonely square and would make a darkness even at noon. A few steps from St. Michael's will bring you to a relic of a different kind, fraught with widely different associations — the birthplace of the pious poet Isaac Watts. The house stands in French street, a little back from the sidewalk, on the east side, and is a two-story red-brick dwelling, having eight windows in the front of it and two doors. Between the house and the street there is a garden which was brilliant with the blazing yellow of a mass of blooming marigolds. A tall iron fence encloses the garden, within which are six poplar trees growing along the margin, and if you stand at the gate and look along French street you can discern Southampton Water, at no great distance. They venerate the memory of Dr.

B

Watts in this town, and they have not only
built a church in his honour, just above
Bar Gate, but have set up his statue (by
Mr. Lucas) in the park, — the figure of the
apostolic bard as he appeared when in the
act to preach. That piece of sculpture —
the pedestal of which is faced with medal-
lions illustrative of the life and labours of
the bard — was appropriately dedicated by
the Earl of Shaftesbury, in July 1861.
Leaving the birthplace of Watts you have
only to turn a neighbouring corner and pro-
ceed a short distance to find an effect of
contrast still more remarkable — the remnant of the Domus Dei, in Winkle street,
the burial-place of the decapitated nobles,
Scrope, Gray, and Cambridge, who lost their
lives for conspiracy to assassinate King
Henry V. This was an almshouse in
Henry's day and later [it was founded in
the reign of Richard I.], but only the
chapel of it remains, and that has been
restored — a small, dark, oblong structure,
partly Norman and partly Early English.
Queen Elizabeth assigned that church for
the use of Protestant refugees who fled
from the persecution of the tyrant Alva —
so active in the Low Countries from 1567
to 1573. Service is still performed in it,

in the French language. Under the chancel
floor of that old edifice rest the ashes of the
false friends [dismissed to their death
nearly five centuries ago] who would have
slain their king and imperilled their country ; and upon the south wall, near the
altar, there is a tablet of gray stone, with
indented, blackened letters, bearing this
record of their fate :

RICHARD, EARL OF CAMBRIDGE,
LORD SCROPE OF MASHAM,
SIR THO. GRAY OF NORTHUMBERLAND,
CONSPIRED TO MURDER KING
HENRY V. IN THIS TOWN AS HE
WAS PREPARING TO SAIL WITH HIS
ARMY AGAINST CHARLES THE SIXTH,
KING OF FRANCE, FOR WHICH
CONSPIRACY THEY WERE EXECUTED
AND BURIED NEAR THIS PLACE
IN THE YEAR
MCCCCXV.

As you stand by that sepulchre you will
remember with a new interest and emotion
the noble, pathetic speech — as high a
strain of pure eloquence and lofty passion
as there is in our language — with which
Shakespeare makes the heroic prince de-
plore and rebuke, at the same instant, the

treachery of the friendship in which he had
entirely believed and trusted. Those lords
were beheaded just outside of Bar Gate.
Near their tomb, leaning against the wall,
is a beautiful old brass, — the full-length
figure of a French cleric of the time of
Queen Elizabeth, — mounted upon an oak
board; the head being carved in marble,
while the person is of the dark green hue
that old brasses so often acquire, and that
seems to enhance at once their interest and
their opulent effect.

In Southampton, as indeed all over England, the disposition to preserve the relics
of a romantic past is stronger at present than
it was a hundred years ago; and for this
the antiquary has reason to be deeply grateful. His constant regret, indeed, is that
this gentle impulse did not awaken earlier.
The old Castle of Southampton [where King
Stephen reigned, who "was a worthy peer"]
was long ago destroyed; but fragments of
the walls remain, and these, it is pleasant
to observe, are guarded with scrupulous
care. As you stroll along the shore your
gaze will wander from the gay and busy
steamboats, — alert for the channel islands
and for France, and seeming like brilliant
birds that plume their wings for flight, —

and will rest on grim towers and bastions
of the thirteenth and the fifteenth centuries,
over which the ivy hangs in dense draperies
of shining emerald, and against which the
copious flowers of geranium and nasturtium
blaze in scarlet and gold. One of those cit-
adels, peacefully occupied now by the Harbour Board, bears record of a time, in 1482,
when gunpowder was used there, to repel
a night attack made by the French; so that
the American pilgrim, upon this spot, is
usefully reminded that there were lively
times in the world even before Columbus
made his interesting discovery. A straggling procession of belated travellers, bearing bags, rushed wildly by, as I stood before
that gray remnant of feudal magnificence,
and an idle youth in the gateway, happily
furnished with a flageolet, gayly performed
upon it "The girl I left behind me."
Nothing can exceed, in mingled strange-
ness and drollery, the use of these quaint
places for the business and the pleasure of
the passing hour. Roaming through the
narrow little squalid thoroughfare of Blue
Anchor lane, amid the picturesque foundations of what was once the royal palace
of John and of Henry III., — now a mass of
masonry that has outlasted the storms and

ravages of a thousand years, — I looked
into dingy lodging-houses that are scarcely
more than holes in a wall, and threaded a
difficult way among groups of ragged children, silenced for a moment by the presence
of a stranger, but soon loud again in their
careless frolic over the crumbling grandeur
of forgotten kings.   Blue Anchor lane
leads to the Arcade in the west wall of the
city, which, with its nineteen splendid
arches, is surely as fine a specimen of true
Norman architecture as could be found in
this kingdom.   Bar Gate, at the top of the
High street, is also a noble relic of Norman
taste and skill; but Bar Gate has been
somewhat modernised by changes and restoration ; and the statue, upon its south
front, of George III. in the dress of a
Roman Emperor, mars its venerable antiquity with a touch of unconsciously comic
humour.

Many excursions are practicable from
Southampton.   One of the prettiest of them
is the drive westward, by the Commercial
road and Romsey lane, to the village of
Millbrook, where there is an old church, and
where — in the adjacent cemetery — an obe-
lisk of granite marks the resting-place of
the poet Robert Pollock, author of *The*

Course of Time — a poem much read and admired by pious people sixty years ago. Another, which may better be made on foot, is the ramble along the avenue to Southampton Common, and so, beneath oaks, elms, and lime-trees, and through "a sweet disorder" of shrubbery and gorse, to the beautiful cemetery in which hawthorns, evergreens, and a profusion of all the flowers that grow in this radiant land have made a veritable bower for the awful silence and inscrutable majesty of death.   I wandered there to look upon the burial-place of my old friend Edward Sothern, and I came upon it, in an afternoon that was all sunshine and fragrance, — like those days of careless mirth that once we knew together.   There never was a droller or more whimsical spirit. There never was a comedian who to the faculty of eccentric humour added a more subtle power of intellectual perception and artistic purpose.   Few players of our time have made so much laughter or given so much innocent pleasure.   But he could not bear prosperity, and he lived too much for enjoyment — and so, prematurely, his bright career ended.   A simple cross of white marble marks the place of his last sleep and the leaves of a sturdy oak rustle over his head ; and as I turned away from that place of peace I saw the shimmering roses all around, and heard the cawing of the rooks in the distant elms, and felt and knew that in this slumber there are no dreams and that with the dead all is well.

Artemas Ward died in Southampton: Edward Sothern is buried there. It seems but yesterday since those lords of frolic were my companions ; but the grass has long been growing over them and even the echo of their laughter has died away. Historic association dignifies a place ; but it is the personal association that makes it familiar. From Southampton the Pilgrim Fathers, nearly three hundred years ago, sailed away to found another England in the western wild. Innumerable legends of that kind haunt the town and hallow it. Yet to one dreamer its name will ever, first of all, bring back the slumberous whisper of leaves that ripple in a summer wind and the balm of flowers that breathe their blessing on a comrade's rest.

II.

PAGEANTRY AND RELICS.

A PLEASANT course, if you would drift from the channel coast into the Midlands, is to go from Southampton, by either Winchester or less directly by Salisbury, to Basingstoke, and thence northward by Reading and Oxford. Another good way — which has been mine — is to loiter slowly along the west of England, taking the track of the cathedral towns, and viewing whatever of historic interest may be observed in those places and in the pleasant and memorable regions that environ them. There should be no inexorable route, — for the chief charm of English travel is liberty of caprice ; and whichever way you turn you are sure to find some peculiar beauty that will reward your quest. My path (July 1891) has traversed Salisbury, Amesbury, Stonehenge, Glastonbury, Wells, Cheddar, Bristol, Gloucester, Worcester, and Evesham ; and all the while it has seemed to wind through a fairy realm of flowers and of dreams. Each part of England has its charming peculiarities, but the general characteristics of English scenery are uniform. The cities are the workshops: the rest is one great garden of diversified and ever-changing beauty. As you range through the country you gaze on wooded hills in the glimmering distance, dark or bright beneath skies of rain or sun — never one thing long, but always fickle, like a capricious girl whose loveliness is the more bewitching because unsure. Green fields fill the foreground, in which cattle are grazing and sheep are couched beneath the trees. Here and there a stately manor-house gleams from its lordly grove. Little cottages, picturesque with roofs of thatch and with tiny latticed windows, nestle by the roadside. Some of the fields have just been gleaned and ploughed, so that the bare earth, in rich brown squares, affords a lively contrast with meadows of brilliant grass and masses of rippling barley. Now and then you see a comely mare, with her awkward little colt, reposing in the shadow of a copse. Yellow haystacks, artfully trimmed, attract the eye, and circular clumps of trees upon the hill-slopes attest the wise, prescient care of the

gardeners of long ago. The land is gently
undulating and in the valleys there are rows
of pollard willows, by which you may trace
the current of a hidden stream. Far away,
or near at hand sometimes, suddenly appears
a gray spire or a grim tower, suggesting a
thought of monastic seclusion or a reminiscence of historic antiquity. White roads,
often devoid for many miles equally of vehicles and pedestrians, wind through the level
plains and over the ridges of lonely hills.
Rivers gleam in the landscape, some rapid
and some tranquil. Rain-clouds drift frequently over the scene, but only serve to
make it more sweetly beautiful. The past
and the present are softly blended in a gentle pageant of wood and meadow, park and
common, church and castle, lawn and pasture, clouds that are like cloth of bronze, and
earth that is clad in emerald and scarlet;
while over the broad expanse of this various
loveliness, in which the fresh garlands of
Nature deck with perennial bloom the
crumbling relics of an historic architectural
grandeur that is dead and gone, the skies of
summer brood with a benediction of peace.

It is the natural desire for change of
scenery that prompts an Englishman to
visit other lands; but he can find no other

land that is as rich as his own in those
treasures of suggestion which are the chief
gain of travel. One picture of the old familiar Shakespeare country may stand for
many that are constantly within his reach.
A spiral stair of forty-five steps gives access,
for the adventurous explorer, to the ring-
ing-loft of the tower of Stratford church,[1]
and a ladder of nineteen rounds will then
conduct him to the bell-chamber above.
He may climb further if he likes to do so,
and ascend into the interior of the stone
spire. This is not the oak spire, covered
with lead, that Shakespeare saw, but one
that replaced it in 1746. From the ring-
ing-loft a small portal will give egress to
the chancel roof. In all directions the
prospect from the tower is beautiful.
Looking westward along the nave, the observer will view a considerable part of the
old town, — the slate roofs of its thick-
clustering, red-brick dwellings wet with
recent rain and shining in the fitful sunlight, — and beyond it the bold crest and

[1] In the winding stair that leads to the top of the
great tower of Warwick Castle there are one hundred
and thirty-three steps. In the spiral that leads to
the top of the tower of St. Mary's church, Warwick,
there are one hundred and sixty.

green slopes of Borden hill, where "the
wild thyme" grows in sweet luxuriance,
and where, since it is close to Shottery, the
poet, as he strolled with his sweetheart in
those distant days when love was young,
possibly may have found (as many Shake-
speareans think he did) the fragrant "bank"
of the *Midsummer Night's Dream.*   Southward stands the crag-like hill of Meon, once
a stronghold of the Danes, and far away
the lonely Broadway tower looms faintly
on the ridge of its emerald highland.
Further still and still more dimly visible is
the wavering outline of the Malvern hills.
In the north, weltering beneath the sombre
rain-clouds of retreating storm, are the
green heights of Welcombe, where once the
Saxons had a fortified camp ; while near at
hand you see the turrets of the Shakespeare
Memorial ;   stately   Avonbank with its
wealth of various trees and its flower-
spangled terraces ; and the old churchyard
of Stratford, in which the roses bloom freely
over man's decay, and in which the gray,
lichen-covered stones are cold and forlorn
against the brilliant green of the sun-smit-
ten sod.   A wide stretch of dark emerald
meadow, intersected with long, dense hedgerows of hawthorn and wild honeysuckle,

fills the near prospect, in the east, while
gently sloping hills extend into the distance
beyond, some wooded and some bare, and
all faintly enwreathed with silver mist. At
the base of the tower flows the Avon, its
dark waters wrinkled by the breeze. Rooks
are cawing over Avonbank. Swifts and
swallows are twittering around the spire.
The leafy boughs of those great elms
that engirdle Shakespeare's church toss
and rustle in the strong wind. Sudden
shafts of sunlight illumine the lovely
pageant, far and near, and soon the glory
of the west fades into that tender gloaming
which is the crowning charm of the English
summer day. There is no need to roam
far afield when you can gaze upon scenes at
home that are at once so lovely to the vision
and so enchanting with association for the
imaginative mind.

III.

THE SHAKESPEARE CHURCH.

THE renovation of the Shakespeare church has not (July 1891) been completed; but only a few old things in it remain to be destroyed, and no doubt the final strokes will be delivered within a short time. The glory and the grandeur of that old church cannot, indeed, be entirely despoiled, even by the superserviceable zeal of bigotry and the regulative spirit of button-making convention. Something of venerable majesty must still survive in the gray, mossy stones of that massive tower and in the gloomy battlements of nave and chancel through which the winds of night sigh sadly over Shakespeare's dust. The cold sublimity of the ancient fabric, with its environment of soft and gentle natural beauty and its associations of poetic renown, can never be wholly dispelled. Almost everything has been done, however, that could be done to make the place modern and conventional.

The appearance of the church, especially of its interior, has been materially changed. A few of the changes were, perhaps, essential, and those may have been made wisely; and all of the changes have been made with mechanical skill if not always with taste. A few more touches, and the inside of the ancient building will be as neat and prim as a box of candles. That was the avowed object of the restoration — to make the church appear as it used to appear when it was built and before it had acquired any association whatever; and that object has been measurably accomplished. But all change here was an injury.

When all is over and old things have been made new the devotees of Shakespeare may be asked what it is of which they think they have reason to complain. Their answer is ready. They wanted to have the church repaired; they did not want to have it rebuilt. Alteration was unnecessary and it was wrong. The Shakespeare church is a national monument. More than that — it is a literary shrine for all the world. There was an indescribable poetic charm about the old edifice, which had been bestowed upon it not by art but by time. That charm needed only to be left untouched. Nothing should ever have been done to dispel it. The building had acquired character. It had become venerable with age, storied with association, and picturesque with quaintness. The suns and the storms of centuries had left their traces on its walls. The actions and sufferings, the inspirations and eccentricities of successive generations had impressed themselves upon its fabric. It had been made individual and splendid, — like a visage of some noble old saint of mediæval times, a face lined and seamed with thought, dignified with experience, sublimated with conquered passion. Above all, it had enshrined, for nearly three hundred years, the ashes of the greatest poet — and therefore the greatest benefactor of humanity — that ever lived. All that was asked was that it should be left alone. To repair it in certain particulars became a necessity; but to alter it was to do it an irreparable harm. That harm has been done; and it is that which the Shakespeare scholar resents and deplores; and he is right to do so.

I lately went into the chancel and stood there alone, in front of the altar, and looked around — in amazement and sorrow. The aspect of that chancel is no longer ancient;

it is new. The altar has been moved from its place against the east wall, beneath the great window, and has been elevated upon a double pedestal. The floor around it has been paved with encaustic tiles, of hideous brown and yellow. Almost all the mural tablets upon the north and south walls have been carried away, and they may now be found dispersed in the transepts, while their place is to be filled with a broad expanse of wooden panels, extending from the backs of the miserere stalls upward to the sills of the windows. The stalls themselves have been repaired — but this was necessary, because the wooden foundations of them had become much decayed. And, finally, the stone screens that filled half of the window back of Shakespeare's monument and half of the window back of the busts of Judith Combe and her lover[1] have been removed. The resultant effect — which would be excellent in a modern hotel but which is detestable

[1] Judith Combe died in August 1649, — just prior to her purposed marriage, — " in ye armes of him who most entirely loved and was beloved of her, even to ye very death." She belonged, no doubt, to the family of John-a-Combe, who died July 10, 1614, and whose tomb is at the north side of the chancel window of the Shakespeare church. The tomb at the south side is that of James Kendal, 1751.

here — is the effect of enterprise and novelty. The pervading air is that of the
new broom and the modern improvements.
Those improvements, no doubt, are fine ;
but if ever there was a place on earth where
they are inappropriate that place is the
Shakespeare church. They suit well with
it as a place of ecclesiastical ritual, and if
the church were merely that nobody would
greatly care even if it were made as bright
as a brass band. But since it is the literary
shrine of the world no one who appreciates
its value can fail to regret that the ruthless
hand of innovation has been permitted to
degrade it, in any degree whatever, to the
level of the commonplace.

When Dean Balsall (obiit 1491) built
the chancel of that church, about four
hundred years ago (1480), he placed it
against a little stone building, the remnant
of an ancient monastery — as good antiquarian scholars believe — which was long used
as the priest's study and under which was
a charnel house or crypt. [A great mass
of human bones was removed from that
crypt about 1886, and buried in a pit in the
churchyard.] The stone screen in the
lower half of the Shakespeare window was
necessary as a part of the sustaining wall

between the old structure and the new one,
and later it was found useful as a back-
ground for the Shakespeare monument.
Against that screen the bust of the poet
was placed by his children and his friends,
and as they saw it and knew it and left it,
so it should have been preserved and per-
petuated. So until this period it has remained; but the pilgrim to Stratford church
hereafter will never see the bust of Shakespeare as it was seen by his daughters. A
link that bound us to the past has been
severed and no skill of man can now avail
to restore it. Back of the bust has been
placed a stained window, commemorative
of J. O. Halliwell-Phillipps, the renowned
Shakespeare scholar. This was put in on
July 27, 1891, late in the afternoon; and
that same night it was my fortune to have
a view of it, from within and from without.
The light of the gloaming had not yet
faded. The bell-ringers were at practice in
the tower, and the sweet notes of the *Blue
Bells of Scotland* were wafted downward in
a shower of silver melody upon the still ai.'
of haunted chancel and darkening nave.
Enough of light yet lingered to display the
fresh embellishment, and I examined it
closely and viewed it for a long time. It

is exceedingly ugly — being prosaic in design and coarse in colour. The principal
object in its composition is the head of a
bull which, engirt with flames, rests upon
a heap of stones, encircled with a rivulet
of ultramarine blue. Upon each side, in
contrasted groups, stand several figures,
two or three of them visible at full length,
but most of them visible only in part. Of
human heads the picture contains eleven.
The chief colours are blue, purple, bronze,
scarlet, and gray. The action of the principal figures is spirited and the treatment of
the faces shows artistic skill — those qualities of charm being the merits of the work.
As a memorial, the window means nothing, while its implied reference to one of
the stories of Jewish history is completely
unimportant. The inscription is from the
Bible: "And with the stones he built an
altar in the name of the Lord." The meaning of this is figurative and it is reverent
and irreproachable. Yet the observer who
reads that sentence can scarcely repress a
smile when he remembers that the stones
which were taken from the Shakespeare
window, to make room for this pretentious
deformity, now form a channel for hot-air
pipes under the chancel floor. It is some-

thing, however, that they were put to use, and not treated as rubbish.

The necessity for saving a relic here and there seems not to have been ignored. The stone reading-desk that long adorned this church was sold to a stone-mason in the Warwick road ; the top of the stone pulpit was thrown away ; but the broken and battered font, at which possibly the poet was baptized, has been placed upon the pillar that formerly supported the stone pulpit, and this structure may now be seen in the southwest corner of the nave. There also have been placed the three carved canopies of stone that formerly impended over the sedalia in the chapel of Thomas a' Becket, — now occupied by the organ works. In the south transept stand two large gravestones, the memorials of former vicars, which were removed from the chancel — where they ought to have been left. The lately discovered (1890) gravestone of Judith Combe has been placed in the chancel floor, beneath her bust. In making repairs, the vault of Dean Balsall, which is close to that of Shakespeare, was broken open, and it was inspected if not explored — but the remains were not disturbed. Let us be properly thankful for

so much forbearance.   The time was when
the present vicar of Stratford, Rev. George
Arbuthnot, gave his consent that the grave
of Shakespeare might be opened ; [1] and there
are uneasy spirits still extant whom inquis-
itive curiosity would quickly impel to that
act of desecration.   Whatever remnant survives, therefore, of the spirit of reverence
in the ecclesiastical authority of Stratford
ought to be prized and cherished.

[1] Readers who wish to know why it is thought by
some people that the grave of Shakespeare ought to
be explored will find dubious reasons set forth in a
curious and interesting book called *Shakespeare's
Bones*, written by C. M. Ingleby, LL.D., 1883.   Dr.
Ingleby has collected many striking facts with regard
to the explorations of other hallowed tombs.   He
appears to think it probable that the relics of Shakespeare have already been rifled : but this is conjec-
ture.   His assertion that a fresh stone was laid over
Shakespeare's grave not much more than fifty years
ago is not supported by any authority that I can find.

IV.

A STRATFORD CHRONICLE.

THE old Guild Hall and Grammar School
of Stratford is to be restored. This
good work was begun in 1891 by Charles
Edward Flower, the chief benefactor of
Shakespeare's town. The exterior of that
building was covered with plaster in 1786.
It is purposed to remove the plaster and
expose the ancient timbers, whereby the
picturesque aspect of the structure will
be greatly enhanced. The building, however, will not be altered; it will only
be relieved of disfigurements that were
foisted upon it in comparatively recent
times. Those disfigurements include the
panelling of the interior, beneath which, no
doubt, will be discovered some remains of
antique decoration. At the south end of
the hall traces have already been observed
of what may once have been a fresco of the
Crucifixion. On the walls of the council
chamber, now occupied by the head-master

of the Grammar School, two frescoes of
large roses were recently discovered — em-
blems that possibly were placed there to com-
memorate the happy ending of the Wars
of the Roses, in August 1485, three years
after the formal foundation of the school of
Thomas Jolyffe.[1] One interesting relic of
the Shakespeare period, and indeed of a
much earlier period, must be sacrificed —
the cottage, in the rear of the hall, which
is known as the schoolmaster's house, and
in which lived Walter Roche,[2] who is believed to have been Shakespeare's teacher.
That cottage has greatly suffered beneath
the ravages of time, and it is now a total
wreck. The chapel of the Guild needs res-

---

[1] The Rev. Mr. Laffan says that the school existed
in embryo as early as 1412, and that a new house for
its accommodation was erected by the Guild of the
Holy Cross in 1427. The estate of the Guild was
confiscated by Henry VIII., but the school was re-
established by Edward VI. in 1553, and since that
time it has been called The King's New School, or
King Edward VI. Grammar School. The building was repaired and decorated in 1568. The boy
Shakespeare, it is believed, began to attend the
school in 1571.

[2] The signature of Walter Roche, exceedingly
rare, is on a deed dated 1578, relative to a tenement
in Ely street, Hereford, preserved in the astonishing
and precious collection made by the late J. O. Halliwell-Phillipps.

toration and probably soon will receive it;
but when that sacred edifice is touched the
most reverent care will be taken to preserve
unchanged the aspect of venerable majesty
that long has made it one of the most impressive churches in England. The clergyman who presides over the Guild chapel is
the head-master of the Grammar School, the
Rev. R. S. De Courcy Laffan, — a scholar,
a Shakespearean, a man of feeling and
taste; and it is certain that no desecration
will be permitted by him. The church of
Shakespeare's sepulchre has been marred.
The church associated with his school-days
will be scrupulously preserved.

Joseph Skipsey, the Newcastle poet, who
in the summer of 1889 succeeded Miss
Maria Chataway as custodian of the Shakespeare Birthplace, resigned that office and
withdrew from it in October 1891. No
true successor to the Chataway sisters has
been found, or is likely to be found, for the
office of custodian of that venerable house.
The Chataway sisters retired from their
post in June 1889, after seventeen years
of service. The elder, Miss Maria Chataway, who officially held the place, was over
seventy-eight years old; the younger, Miss
Caroline Chataway, her assistant, was sev-

enty-six. It was Miss Caroline who usually
escorted the visitor through the principal
rooms, and who told, in such a quaintly
characteristic way, the story of the building
as a relic of Shakespeare days : and it seems
not likely that anybody else will ever tell
the tale so well. The Chataway sisters, on
leaving the Shakespeare Birthplace, took up
their residence in a cottage in the Warwick road. Miss Maria Chataway died on
January 31, 1891.

The trustees of the Shakespeare Birthplace were authorized by an act of Parliament, March 16, 1891, to use, for the
purchase of other Shakespeare property,
whatever surplus of money had accumulated
in their possession. They have bought, for
£3000, the Anne Hathaway cottage, which
was the home of the poet's wife, and they
intend to buy the Mary Arden cottage, at
Wilmcote, which was the home of the poet's
mother. Mrs. Mary Taylor Baker continues
to reside in the Hathaway house and to
show the wainscot, the great timbers, the
antique bedstead, the dresser, the settle,
and the fire-place with which it is believed
that Shakespeare and his Anne were long
and happily familiar. Mrs. Baker's pedigree,
as the descendant and representative of the

Hathaway family of Shakespeare's time, is set down as follows in her old family Bible : —

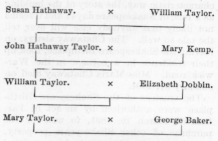

Susan Hathaway. × William Taylor.

John Hathaway Taylor. × Mary Kemp.

William Taylor. × Elizabeth Dobbin.

Mary Taylor. × George Baker.

The marriage of Mary Taylor to George Baker occurred in 1840. The Susan Hathaway who stands at the head of this pedigree is understood to have been Anne Hathaway's niece.

There are credulous persons who believe in what is called the Ely Palace Portrait of Shakespeare. Mr. Henry Graves, long noted as a connoisseur of art and as one of the best authorities in the kingdom as to such a matter, believes in it and he has been heard to say that he would value the painting at five hundred guineas or at any fancy price above that figure. The Ely

Palace Portrait of Shakespeare was discovered in London and was bought by Bishop Turton, of Ely, in 1846. It purports to have been an heirloom in a family resident in Little Britain, and personally known to Shakespeare, and the story of it declares that it was painted in Shakespeare's time. In contour and expression it bears some resemblance to the Dreshout likeness. The face, however, is thin and pale and the eyes are small. In May 1891 this portrait was, for the first time in many years, taken out of its frame, in order that the glass might be cleaned, and then was observed the following inscription upon the left-hand upper corner of the canvas: "AE. 39. ✕ 1603." Its existence had not before been known at the Birthplace, but subsequent inquiry has ascertained that the inscription was known to Bishop Turton when he bought the picture, and doubtless it had an effect upon his judgment of its authenticity. The Ely Palace Portrait is preserved at the Birthplace, where it is an interesting feature in the collection that was made for the museum department by William Oakes Hunt and J. O. Halliwell-Phillipps.

Among Shakespeare relics that long survived in Stratford, but now have disap-

peared, was the old house of Avonbank.
That building stood next to the principal
gate of Trinity churchyard, on land that
now forms part of the estate of Charles
Edward Flower, and it was designated, in
the town records, "the House of St. Mary
in old town." Thomas Green, who has
been variously styled "the poet's cousin"
and "the poet's intimate friend," — he was
town-clerk of Stratford from 1614 to 1617, —
lived there, and accordingly it is reasonable
to suppose that the house may have been
one of Shakespeare's habitual resorts. Each
room in it had a name. One was called
"the churchyard room"; one "the bee-
hive"; one "the end"; one "the middle";
and one "the bird's nest."

Another Shakespeare relic that has disappeared is the old Market Cross of Stratford. That structure, often seen by Shakespeare, was surely as old as the early time
of Queen Elizabeth. It stood close by the
southwest corner of High street and Wood
street and was apparently used for a
market. At a meeting of the Common
Council of Stratford, held August 2, 1794,
it was "agreed that the house at the Cross,
late in the possession of Mr. Robert Man-
der, be wholly taken down and laid open to

the road; that Mr. Taylor take down the
house and be careful to put the materials
by for the use of the corporation." So
said, so done. The Cross was taken down
and removed in one day, — Saturday, August
11, 1821, — and its base was finally placed in
the centre walk of the Shakespeare Birthplace garden. The foundation stone of the
ugly market-house now standing at the junc-
tion of Wood street and Henley street was
laid by George Morris, Mayor of Stratford,
on the coronation day of George IV.

Charles Edward Flower's Memorial theatre edition of Shakespeare's plays includes
the thirty-seven plays and fills eight volumes.
This edition is intended equally for the actor
and the reader. Each play is printed in
full, but while the text that is spoken on the
stage is given in brevier, the passages that
are usually omitted are given in minion.
The text is genuine, and the editorial
work has been done with scholarship, taste,
veneration, and patient zeal. In several
cases Mr. Flower was obliged to make new
stage versions — notably in those of *The
Two Gentlemen of Verona*, *Love's Labour's
Lost*, *The Comedy of Errors*, and the first
part of *Henry VI*. Those new versions
have been acted at the Memorial theatre,

and without exception they were successful. The edition was printed by George Boyden, at the Stratford *Herald* press.

The library of the Shakespeare Memorial now contains 6260 volumes. There are 236 English editions of Shakespeare in that collection. Among the relics that have been obtained are the manuscript of the late Charles Mackay's treatise on *Obscure Words in Shakespeare's Plays*, and a human skull that was used as "Yorick's skull, the king's jester," by John Philip Kemble and by Edmund Kean, when playing Hamlet. The store of relics in Stratford is naturally considerable, and many of them are of great interest. An uncommonly fine autograph of Robert Burns is owned by Mr. William Hutchings, of this town, and the original manuscript of the letter that Dr. Johnson addressed (June 26, 1777) to Dr. Dodd, the forger, then under sentence of death, is one of the possessions of Alderman Bird.

Robert Bell Wheler,[1] the historian of Stratford, was buried in Trinity churchyard, together with several of his relatives. We

---

[1] An autograph letter from Robert Bell Wheler has come into my possession, which is interesting not only as a relic of the historian but because of a

are soon forgotten when we are dead,—as intimated by poor old Rip Van Winkle, — and the burial-place of the venerable antiquary is fast hastening to decay. The graves of the Wheler family are enclosed within a tall iron fence and over them the grass grows thick and wild. A double stone marks the spot, on which is the following inscription : —

---

reference that it makes to one of the most distinguished names in recent American history. It is addressed to the antiquary John Gough Nichols, F.S.A., No. 25 Parliament-st., London.

"Dear Sir: Mr. Sumner, an American gentleman to whom I was last summer introduced by a friend of his residing in this place, wishes to inspect Yorkington's Pilgrimage, Mr. S. having, as I understood, visited some of the places mentioned in it. I have taken the liberty of giving him your address, which I trust you will pardon, and I shall feel obliged by your allowing him to inspect the MS. or the copy, but of course not to take either of them out of your possession. And should he desire to make any extracts, I leave that to your wishes, as I hardly know what use you may require to make of the Journal. When you have done with the MS. I shall be happy in receiving it back, with the copy. And I remain, dear sir, very truly yours,

"ROBERT BELL WHELER.

"Stratford-upon-Avon, 31st Decr., 1842.

"Mr. Sumner dates from 38 Duke St., St. James's."

D

In memory of
ROBERT WHELER, Gent.,
Who died
29th August, 1819,
Aged 77 years.

Also of his daughter,
ELIZABETH WHELER,
Who died 29th May, 1852,
Aged 72 years.

In memory of
ROBERT BELL WHELER
(Only son of Robert Wheler)
Who died 15th July, 1857,
Aged 72 years.

Also of ANN WHELER,
Daughter of Robert Wheler,
Who died 13th Sept., 1870,
Aged 87 years.

The historian's mother died at Quinton
and was buried in the churchyard of that
place, on the southeast side of the church —
the stone that marks her sepulchre being
inscribed as follows : —

In memory of
ELIZABETH WHELER,
Wife of Robert Wheler,
Of Stratford-upon-Avon.
She died 13 April, 1786,
Aged 29.

Making a visit to the old city of Gloucester, it was my privilege to see the Shakespeare relics that are preserved there, — in a dwelling in Westgate street, occupied by the family of Fletcher, dealers in fire-arms. Mrs. E. Fletcher, who died in 1890, at an advanced age, claimed to be a collateral descendant from Shakespeare, and she always strenuously maintained that those memorials of the poet, a Jug and a Cane, had been handed down, through succeeding generations, in the family, from Shakespeare's time. The tradition declares that Shakespeare once owned and used those articles, and the religious care with which they have been guarded is a proof that the tradition has not lacked power. Each of them is enclosed in a case of wood and glass, and I found the cases in a locked room. The Jug is made of stone-ware, and is of a simple and usual form, having panelled sides with figures embossed upon them; and it is surmounted with a metal lid. The Cane is a Malacca joint, fully four feet long. As it was enclosed I could not take it into my hands for close examination, but I saw that it is such a cane as was customarily carried in the days of Queen Elizabeth and James I. Miss Fletcher, who showed those relics, spoke of them with veneration, and she dis-

played a large box of papers, both written
and printed, relative to their history.
"They are not now for sale," she said,
"but they will be hereafter." They have
several times been exhibited in public, and
they are always shown to the wanderer who
will take the trouble to inquire for them.
An effigy of Shakespeare looks down upon
them from the wall of the little parlour in
which they are enshrined; and it was easy,
when standing in their presence — in the
ancient and romantic city of Gloucester,
with haunting historic shapes on every hand
— to credit their sanctity as objects that
Shakespeare knew and touched.

_____

DEATH OF CHARLES EDWARD FLOWER.

May 10, 1892. — The death of Charles
Edward Flower is a bereavement to the
town of Stratford-upon-Avon and it deprives
the Shakespeare fraternity of one of its best
friends. Mr. Flower was a native of Stratford-upon-Avon, and he grew up there to be
one of its most respected citizens. He loved
and venerated the name of Shakespeare;
he was solicitous for the credit of his native
place; and he wished that Stratford might
always prove worthy of its association with

the first poet of the world. He possessed
large wealth and he used it freely for the
honour and advancement of his town. He
was the founder of the Shakespeare Memorial: he gave the land on which it stands
and also the greater part of the money
that built it, and he gave and improved and
beautified the gardens by which it is enclosed. The corner-stone of the Memorial
was laid on April 23, 1877, and the building was opened, with a performance of
Much Ado About Nothing, on April 23,
1879. Mr. Flower was constantly adding
books to its library. One of the gifts that
he had in store for it was a set of the four
folios of Shakespeare. He edited the Memorial edition of Shakespeare's plays. He
was active in every good work in Stratford,
and he was respected and beloved by the
whole community. One of the last of his
labours was the restoration of the Guild
Hall and Grammar School of Stratford.
That work of restoration will go on, and
Stratford will soon possess another object
of antique beauty. Whenever a good deed
was to be done his liberality never halted.
Hundreds of Americans who have visited
Stratford will remember his hospitality and
recall with pleasure his kindness, his cheer-

ful sympathy, and the refinements and graces of his beautiful home. Not anywhere in the world remains a more devoted worshipper of Shakespeare, a more practical friend of literature and art, a more public-spirited citizen, or a man of more inflexible principle and sterling integrity. Under an austere demeanour Mr. Flower veiled without being able to conceal tenderness of heart, gentleness of temperament, quick appreciation of merit and of goodness, and a fine sense of humour. He left no children. His widow — in whom his virtues were reflected and increased, and in whom his goodness survives — possesses in her bereavement a sympathy too deep for words.

Mr. Flower was born February 3, 1830, and he was educated at the Grammar School of Stratford — the school of Shakespeare. In 1852 he married Sarah, daughter of Mr. Peter Martineau, of Highbury, Middlesex. He passed his whole life in his native town. He died suddenly, at Warwick, on May 3, 1892, and was buried on May 7, in the Stratford cemetery.

"Your cause of sorrow
Must not be measured by his worth, for then
It hath no end."

V.

FROM LONDON TO DOVER.

CALAIS, FRANCE, August 31, 1891. — It is early morning in London. The rain has been falling all night, and in the gray of the dawn it continues to fall — not now in showers but intermittently and in a cold drizzle. The sky is dark and sullen, and through the humid, misty air the towers and spires of the majestic city loom shadow-like, fantastic, and strange. Pools of water stand here and there in the streaming, slippery streets, which are almost devoid equally of vehicles and pedestrians. The shop-keepers of Kensington have not yet awakened, and as my cab rolls through the solitary highways I see that only in a few places have the shutters been taken from the windows. Victoria is presently reached, where, at this early hour, only a few people are astir, so that the confusion and clamour of British travel have not yet begun. Soon our train rumbles out of the

station and we feel that all personal responsibility has been dropped and that we have
yielded to fate — at least till we reach
Dover. The skies begin to brighten as we
cross the Thames, while, gently ruffled by
the morning breeze, the broad expanse of
the river shows like a sheet of wrinkled
steel. At first we speed among long rows
of houses, all built alike — the monotonous
suburban dwellings of towns such as Wands-
worth and Clapham, with their melancholy
little gardens, all dripping with recent rain,
in which marigolds are beginning to bloom,
and great, heavy sunflowers hang their disconsolate heads. Nothing here seems joyous
except the grass, but this has profited by the
pertinacious rain and is richer and greener
than ever. Presently the gardens and
dwellings grow more opulent. The wind
rises with the advance of day and soon the
dense foliage about the hill and vale of
Herne stirs and rustles in the gladness of
its careless life. Now begins the gentle
pageant of English rural scenery — that
blending of soft colour and quaint, delicate
object, the like of which is nowhere to be
found except in England. Every traveller
will remember, and will rejoice to remember, the elements of that delicious picture —

the open, far-reaching stretches of pasture, level, green, and fragrant ; the beds of many-coloured flowers, flashing on emerald lawns ; the fleecy sheep, the sleek horses, and the comely cattle, grouped or scattered in the fields, some feeding, some ruminant, some in motion, and some asleep ; the deep, lush grass and clover ; the nurseries of fruit-trees ; the flying glimpses of gray church-towers and of shining streams ; and over all the frequent flights of solemn rooks and frolicsome starlings that seem at times almost to make a darkness in the air.

Soon the opulent, aristocratic façade of ancient Dulwich College — at once the memorial and the sepulchre of Shakespeare's friend Edward Alleyne — smiles upon us across the meadows and witches us with thoughts of a memorable past. Leaving Dulwich we run through a long tunnel and in a few moments, dashing across the plain of Penge, we perceive the lofty tower and Olympian fabric of the Crystal Palace shining on the hills of Sydenham. This is a fertile, rolling country, much diversified with hill and valley. All around us the banks are scarlet with innumerable standards of the gorgeous poppy and golden with flowers of the colt's foot, and many

red-roofed farm-houses are momentarily
visible in the green depths of lofty groves.
Our way lies through hop fields now, and
the air is delicious with the zestful perfume
of their blossoms. We traverse beds of
wild fern and of many kinds of underwoods,
and in fields that are divided by hedges of
lovely hawthorn we see many sheaves of
the yellow harvest. Quaint little villages
are passed, each group of cottages nestled
around its gray old church, like children
clustered at a parent's knee. The door-
yards are gay with marigolds. There are
broad patches of clover in copious, fragrant
bloom, and on the distant horizon the green
hills, crowned with dark groves, loom
gloomily under straggling clouds. The
wind blows chill, the sky takes on a cold,
silvery hue, and innumerable starlings, flying low, look like black dots upon the dome
of heaven. Our speed is great, and we
leave long trails of thick, smoky vapour that
melts through the trees and hedges or seems
to sink into the ground. At Sole a lovely
rural region is opened and the sky begins
to smile. Yonder on the hillside a venerable church-tower shows its grim parapet.
In the opposite quarter there are hills, thick
wooded or capped with sheaves of the har-

vest — sadly marred, this autumn, by the
rough weather of as drear an August as
England has known. All the same this
scene keeps its picturesque beauty — the
peace of deep vales in which boughs wave,
streams murmur, and stately rooks are
seeking their food ; the peace of old red or
gray farm-houses veiled with ivy and nestled
among flowers. The banks of the Medway
are near at hand and across the crystal
bosom of that beautiful river rises the black
ruin of Rochester castle, flecked with lichen
and haunted by hosts of doves, and near it
the pinnacled tower of Rochester cathedral,
romantic in itself but made more romantic
by the art of the great genius who loved it
so well. Here Dickens laid the scene of
his exquisite story of *Edwin Drood*, and
not far away from this spot stands the old,
lonely house of Gadshill in which he died.
The little town of Rochester is all astir.
The wet, red roofs of its cosy dwellings
glisten in the welcome though transient
sunshine, and on some of those houses
great mantles of green ivy sway gently in
the rising wind. The river is full of ship-
ping, — small craft and steamboats, — and
the gaze of the pilgrim dwells delighted on
brown sails, and tapering spars, and gay

smoke-stacks, and the busy little boats that seem never at rest. Not many views in England possess such animation as pervades the spectacle of the valley of the Medway at Rochester, and the lover of Dickens may well look upon it with affection and leave it with regret.

We dash through a ravine of chalkstone now and have a fine prospect of martial Chatham, which is built in a valley but extends up the side of the adjacent eastward hill; and through one of its long highways our glance follows the plunging flight of a large flock of frightened sheep. At New-Brompton there are many small gray houses and there is a great profusion of red and yellow flowers. A wide reach of glistening water is presently seen, toward the east — which is the Medway, nearing the sea. Harvest fields extend almost to its verge and the country is level for miles — a marsh-land intersected with channels and pools. Presently we come again into hop-fields and we recognise the rich and blooming land of Kent. At Newington there are gloomier skies and dashes of sudden rain, but the grass is thickly strewn with sumptuous white daisies, and the prospect of a noble antique church, with plenteous moss and lichen on its triple-gabled roof and with its square tower bosomed in foliage, would make any gazer forget the weather and cast all discomfort to the winds. Speeding past Sittingbourne you note the breezy activity of that thrifty place, the newly built manufactories, the tall, smoking chimneys, the fine mill, and the miller's still finer dwelling — so close to the brink of his great pond that not the building only but the innumerable flowers that grow around it are reflected in the broad, gleaming pool. This sweet picture passes in an instant, and then, under rifts of blue in a sky of silver, come more of the drenched sheaves of the injured harvest. There is a vision of roads that are full of mire; of glowing hop-fields; of haystacks and thatched cottages; of distant spires peeping out among the trees; of windmills on the hill-tops; of harvesters gathering grain; and of happy children that wave a greeting from poppy-spangled fields. Faversham now, and across the green levels, far away, rise the brown sails of barges and of other little vessels that ply the neighbouring sea. Near at hand the green hedges are full of white and red and yellow flowers, and many sheep are nibbling in the pastures or gazing with

a comic wooden stare at our flying train.
The sky continually changes, and here it is a
dome of dark-gray and silver, across which,
with astonishing speed, thin fleeces of rain-
cloud career on the stormy wind.   We are
come into a beautiful valley, green on all
sides and softly diversified with windmills,
cottages, little gray churches, massive cones
of golden hay, clumps of larch, lines of
delicate silver birch, and large masses of
fragrant hops — the thick vines of which
hang so near that we can almost clutch
their pendant blossoms as we pass.   A veil
of dim sunshine is cast over this verdurous
scene, and as the vale broadens you may
perceive a dazzling variety of objects —
manor-house and cottage, grove and plain,
fields that are brown and fields that are
yellow, thin white roads that wind away
over hill-tops and are lost in the distance,
a bright and rapid stream that flashes
through the meadow, and, grandly crowning the pageant and consecrating its beauty,
the stately and splendid towers of Canterbury cathedral.   There they stand, majestic and glorious, with a thousand years of
history upon their hallowed battlements,
serene, predominant, and changeless amid
the changes of a transitory and vanishing

world. Nothing of architectural creation can excel in charm the spiritual loveliness of that cathedral. York and St. Paul's and Lincoln surpass it in massive grandeur; Gloucester surpasses it in romance; Durham is more rugged and more savagely splendid; Westminster is more rich with poetic association and with ecclesiastical ornament; Ely possesses a greater variety of blended architectural styles and of eccentric character; but, travel where you may, you never will behold a church more completely radiant with the investiture of celestial sublimity. It won my heart years ago, and no one of its magnificent rivals has ever allured me from its shrine.

There is no pause. Berkesbourne flashes by — its velvet plains slumbering under spacious elms and its fields of silken oat-grass blazing with poppies. All about Adisham the thatched cottages and the sheep in the pastures make a pretty picture of smiling content. The harvest is partly mown and partly erect. Rooks and small birds abound, and there are many patches of woodland near by, and many vacant plains. Now and then we run through deep ravines in the chalk. The country is hilly as we approach the sea, and on the gentle acclivities, here

and there, is seen a manor-house, quaint
with gables and latticed casements and
draped with ivy. In the foreground are
fields of clover, and looking beyond those
your gaze falls upon wooded vales in which
the dark sheen of the copper-beech shows
boldly against the green of the elms. A
little graveyard gleams for a moment on
the hillside, — in mute token that Death
also has his part in these scenes of fertile
beauty, — and then we flit through the dark
tunnel and come slowly to a pause beneath
the noble cliffs of Dover. Nothing seems
changed upon this romantic shore since
those far-distant days when first I saw it.
The sombre castle still frowns upon its crag.
The great hillsides are solitary in the bleak
light. The little cabin and the signal-stand-
ard keep, as of old, their lonely vigil on
the wind-beaten summit of the Shakespeare
cliff. The massive stone pier, like a giant's
arm, stretches into the sea and braves its
power and defies its wrath. And on the
vacant, desolate beach the endless surges
still murmur their mysterious, everlasting
dirge — the requiem of broken vows, and
blighted hope, and all the vain and futile
ambitions, passions, and sorrows of mankind. The sea is wild, as our bark springs

into its embrace ; the sky is full of white
and slate-coloured clouds broken into frequent rifts of blue ; and the distant waves
roll up in great purple masses crowned with
plumes of silver. Many shapes of sails are
visible on the distant horizon, and the air
is so clear that I discern at the same moment the high cliffs of Albion and the low-
lying sandhills of France. It is an hour of
memory and of thought ; of dreams and of
visions ; and you forget the common life
that is all around you, — the sailors at their
tasks, the vacant chatter of the tourists, the
clank of the engines, the swirl and strife
of the waters and the winds, — to muse on
old imperial battles that once incarnadined
these seas, and to gaze on the ghostly gal-
leons of the Spanish Armada, the pennons
of the great admirals of Spain and France
and Holland and England, the stately ships
of Raleigh and Drake, of Collingwood and
Rodney and Nelson, and, proudly streaming on the blast, that flag of Britannia which
is still the austere emblem of human freedom, the flag that has

> " Braved, a thousand years,
> The battle and the breeze."

E

VI.

BEAUTIES OF FRANCE.

IT was a beautiful afternoon in summer
when first I saw the shores of France.
The channel, a distressful water when rough,
had been in unusual pleasure, like King
Duncan in the play, so that "observation
with extended view," could look with interest on the Norman coast, as it rose into
sight across the surges. That coast seemed
like the Palisade bank of the Hudson river,
and prompted thoughts of home. It is high
and precipitous and on one of its windy hills
a little chapel is perched, in picturesque
loneliness, east of the stone harbour into
which the arriving steamer glides. At
Dieppe, as at most of the channel ports, a
long pier projects into the sea, and this
was thronged with spectators, as the boat
steamed to her moorings. The road from
Dieppe to Paris passes through Rouen and
up the valley of the Seine. The sky that
day was as blue and sunny as ever it is in

brilliant America; the air was soft and
cool; and the fields of Normandy were
lovely with rich colour and generous with
abundance of golden crops. Now and then
we passed little hamlets, made up of thatched
cottages clustered around a tiny church,
with its sad, quaint place of graves. Sheaves
of wheat were stacked in careless piles in
the meadows. Rows of the tall, lithe Lombardy poplar — so like the willowy girls of
France — flashed by, and rows of the tremu-
lous silver-leaved maple. Sometimes I saw
rich bits of garden ground, gorgeous with
geraniums and with many of the wild-flowers,
neglected, for the most part, in other countries, which the French know so well how
to cultivate and train. In some fields the
reapers were at work; in others women
were guiding the plough; in others the sleek
cattle and shaggy sheep were couched in repose or busy with the herbage; and through
that smiling land the Seine flowed peacefully
down, shining like burnished silver. At
Rouen I saw the round tower and the spires
of the famous cathedral — esteemed one of
the best pieces of Gothic architecture in
Europe; and I thought of Corneille, who
was there born, and of Joan of Arc, who
was there burnt. Just beyond Rouen, on

the east bank of the Seine, the hills take,
and for many miles preserve, the shape of
natural fortifications. Circuitous pathways
wind up the faces of the crags. A chapel
crowns one of the loftiest summits. Cottages
nestle in the vales below. Gaunt windmills
stretch forth their arms, upon the distant
hills. Every rood of the land is cultivated;
and there, as in England, the scarlet poppies
brighten the green, while cosy hedgerows
make the landscape comfortable to the fancy
as well as pretty to the eye, with a sense of
human companionship.

In the gloaming we glided into Paris, and
soon I was driving in the Champs Elysées
and thinking of the Arabian Nights. Nobody can know, without seeing them, how
imperial the great features of Paris are.
My first morning there was a Sunday, and
it was made beautiful by sunshine, singing
of birds, strains of music from passing
bands, and the many sights and sounds
which in every direction bespoke the cheerfulness of the people. I went that day to
a fête in the Bois de Vincennes, where from
noon till midnight a great throng took its
pleasure, in the most orderly, simple, child-
like manner, and where I saw a "picture
in little" of the manners of the French.

It was a peculiar pleasure while in Paris to rise at an early hour and stroll through the markets of St. Honoré, in which flowers have an equal place with more substantial necessities of life, and where order and neatness are perfect. It was impressive, also, to walk in the gardens of the Tuileries, in those lonely morning hours, and to muse over the downfall of the dynasty of Napoleon. Those gardens, formerly the private grounds of the emperor, were open to the public; and streams of labourers, clothed in blue blouses, poured through them every day. But little trace remained of the ravages of the Commune. The Arc de Triomphe stands, in solemn majesty; the Column Vendôme towers toward the sky; the golden figure seems still in act of flight upon the top of the Column of the Bastile. I saw, in the church of Notre Dame, the garments — stained with blood and riddled with bullets — that were worn by the Archbishop of Paris, when he was murdered by the friends of Liberty, Equality, and Fraternity; and I saw, with admiration, a panorama of the siege of Paris, by F. Phillipoteaux, which is a marvel of faithful detail, spirited composition, and the action and suffering of war. But those were all the tokens that I chanced to see of the evil days of France.

The most interesting sights of Paris, to a stranger, are the objects associated with its older history.   Every visitor repairs presently to Les Invalides to see the tomb of Napoleon Buonaparte.   That structure would inspire awe even if it were not associated with that glittering name and that terrible memory.   The gloom of the crypt in which it is sunk ; the sepulchral character of the mysterious, emblematic figures that surround it — " staring right on, with calm eternal eyes " ; the grandeur of the dome that rises above it ; and its own vast size and deathly shape — all those characteristics unite to make it a most impressive object, apart from the solemn sense that in the great, red-sandstone coffin rests, at last, after the stormiest of human lives, the ashes of the most vital man of action who has lived in modern times.   Deeply impressive also are the tombs of Voltaire and Rousseau, in the crypt under the Pantheon. No device more apposite and significant could have been adopted than that which startles you on the front of Rousseau's tomb.   The door stands ajar, and out of it issues an arm and hand, in marble, grasp-

ing a torch. It was almost as if the dead
had spoken with a living voice, to see that
fateful symbol of a power of thought and
passion that never can die, while human
hearts remain human. There is a fine
statue of Voltaire in the vault that holds
his tomb. Those mausoleums are merely
commemorative. The body of Voltaire was
destroyed with quicklime when laid in the
grave, at the Abbey of Celleries, so that it
might not be cast out of consecrated ground.
Other tombs of departed greatness I found
in Père la Chaise. Molière and La Fon-
taine rest side by side. Racine is a neigh-
bour to them. Talma, Auber, Rossini, De
Musset, Desclée, and many other illustrious names, may there be read, in the letters of death. Rachel's tomb is in the
Hebrew quarter of the cemetery — a tall,
narrow, stone structure, with a grated door,
over which the name of RACHEL is graven,
in black letters. Looking through the grat-
ing I saw a shelf on which were vases and
flowers, and beneath it were fourteen im-
mortelle wreaths. A few cards, left by
pilgrims to that solemn shrine of genius
and renown, were upon the floor, and I ven-
tured to add my own, in humble reverence
of genius, to the names which thus gave

homage to the memory of a great actress;
and I gathered a few leaves from the shrubbery that grows in front of her grave. The
famous cemetery is comparatively destitute
of flowers and grass. It contains a few
avenues of trees, but for the most part it is
a mass of ponderous tombs, crowded together upon a hot hill-side, traversed by
little stony pathways sweltering in sun and
dust. No sadder graveyard was ever seen.
All the acute anguish of remediless suffering, all the abject misery and arid desolation of hopeless grief, is symbolised in that
melancholy place. Artisans were repairing
the tomb of Heloïse and Abelard, and this,
for a while, converted a bit of old romance
to modern commonness. Still, I saw the
tomb, and it was elevating to think that
there may be "Words which are things,
hopes which do not deceive."

The most gorgeous modern building in
Paris is the Opera House. No building in
America can vie with it in ornate splendour.
Some observers do but scant justice to the
solid qualities in the French character.
That character is mercurial, yet it contains
elements of stupendous intensity and power;
and this you feel, as perhaps you may never
have felt it before, when you look at such

works as the Opera House, the Pantheon,
the Madeleine, the Invalides, the Louvre,
the Luxembourg, and the miles of stone
embankment that hem in the Seine on both
its sides. The grandest old building in
Paris — also a living witness to French
power and purpose — is the church of Notre
Dame. It will not displace, in the affectionate reverence of Americans, the glory
of Westminster Abbey; but it will fill almost an equal place in their memory. Its
arches are not so grand; its associations are
not so sacred. But it is exceedingly beautiful in forms and in simplicity, and no one
can help loving it; and by reason of its
skilfully devised vistas it is perhaps invested with more of the alluring attribute
of mystery. Some of its associations are
especially impressive. You may there see
the chapel in which Mary Stuart was married to her first husband, Francis II. of
France, and in which Henry VI., of England, was crowned; and you may stand on
the spot on which Napoleon Buonaparte invested himself with the imperial diadem —
which with his own hands he placed on his
own head.[1] I climbed the tower of that

[1] Richard I. of England, at his first coronation,
on September 3, 1189, in Westminster Abbey, took

famous cathedral and at the loftiest attainable height pictured in fancy the awful closing scene of *The Hunchback of Notre Dame*. That romance seemed the truth then, and Claude Frollo, Esmeralda, and Quasimodo were as real as Richelieu. There is a vine growing near the bell-tower and some children were at play there, on the stone platform. I went in beneath the bell and smote upon it with a wooden mallet and heard with pleasure its rich, melodious, soulful music. The four hundred steps are well worn that lead to the tower of Notre Dame. There are few places on earth so fraught with memories; few that so well repay the homage of a pilgrim from a foreign land.

the crown from the altar and delivered it to the archbishop. In both cases the purpose was to signify that the crown was not the gift of the church.

VII.

ELY AND ITS CATHEDRAL.

ELY, CAMBRIDGESHIRE, September 6, 1891. — Gray and sombre London, gloomy beneath vast clouds of steel and bronze, is once more left behind. Old Highgate flits by and we roll through the network of little towns that fills all the space between Hornsey and Tottenham. The country along our course is one of exceptional interest, and but that Buggins the Builder has marred it by making the houses alike it would be one of peculiar beauty. Around Tottenham the dwellings are interspersed with meadows and there are market-gardens and nurseries of flowers, — the bright green of carrot-tops and of the humble but portly cabbage being pleasantly relieved by masses of brilliant hollyhock. Broad fields ensue, — cultivated to the utmost and smiling with plenty; and around some of the houses are beautiful green lawns, divided with hedges of hawthorn. The country, for the most part, is

level, and a fine effect is produced upon the
landscape by single tall trees or by isolated
groups of them, — especially where the plain
slopes gently toward gleaming rivulet and
bird-haunted vale. Everywhere the aspect
is that of prosperity and bloom. The sun
has pierced the clouds and is faintly light-
ing with a golden haze this shadowy summer scene of loveliness and peace. In the
distance are several small streams, dark,
bright, and still, and near them many white
and brown cattle, conspicuous in a sudden
burst of sunshine, are couched under the
trees. A little canal-boat, gayly painted
red and green, winds slowly through the
plain, and over the harvest fields the omni-
present rook wings his solemn flight or
perches on the yellow sheaves. Chingford
has been left to the east, — where you may
explore one of the most picturesque ruined
churches in this country, and where they
show you a hunting-lodge that once was
owned and used by Queen Elizabeth, — and
Enfield has been left to the west where
the nettles grow rank on the low grave of
Charles Lamb, within the shadow of the
grim church-tower that reverberated with
his funeral knell. White Webs has been
passed, with its associations of Father Gar-

net and the Gunpowder Plot, and passed
also is Ponder's End, with its relics and
memories of the baleful Judge Jeffreys.
At Rye House the pilgrim remembers the
plan that was hatched there to murder
Charles II., and thinks of the miserable
death of Lord William Russell upon the
block in Lincoln's Inn Fields. Bishop's
Stortford brings thoughts of the cruel
Bishop Bonner. But the beauty of nature
triumphs over the depravity of man, and
nowhere in this verdant and blooming region is there any hint of a wicked heart or
a sinister action.

The church at Bishop's Stortford crowns
a fine eminence and near that place an old
brick windmill and many black cattle make
a striking picture in the gentle landscape.
The pretty villages of Stanstead and Elsen-
ham glide by, and the wanderer's gaze,
as they pass, rests dreamily on tiny red
cottages with lichened roofs and on the
broad, fertile farms that surround them.
Between Audley End and Cambridge there
is a long stretch of country that contains
only farms and villages, — the cultivation
of the land being thorough and perfect and
the result a picture of contentment and
repose. Presently the region grows more

hilly and under clouds of steel and silver
the landscape is swept by a cool, fragrant
wind, bringing dashes of sudden rain.
Hedges are abundant. Many flocks of
sheep are seen in the pastures. Fine farm-
houses appear and many signs of opulence
are all around them. Wooden windmills
rise picturesque upon the heights, and the
eye rests delightedly on long rows of the
graceful Lombardy poplar. White roads
are visible, here and there, winding away
into the distance, and many kinds of trees
abound ; yet everywhere there is an ample
prospect. At Shelford comes a burst of
sunshine, and looking toward the horizon I
see tall trees that stand like sentinels around
the lovely plain of classic Cambridge,—
where soon I am to wander among such
stately haunts of learning as will fire the
imagination and fill the memory forever
with shapes and scenes and thoughts of
majesty and glory that words are powerless
to tell. But the aspect of Cambridge, as
we glide now along its margin, gives no
hint of the overwhelming magnificence
within its borders. Beyond it, still flying
northward, we traverse a flat country and
see the long roads bowered with trees, the
deep emerald verdure, the banks of white

daisies and red clover, the gardens brilliant with scarlet-runners, sunflowers, and marigolds, the rooks at their customary occupation of feeding, — provident, vigilant, sagacious, and wonderfully humorous, — the artistic forms of the hay-ricks, some circular, some cone-shaped, some square with bevelled edges, and in the long, yellow fields the mowers at their work, some swinging their scythes and some pausing to rest. These and others like them are the labourers whose slow and patient toil, under guidance of a wise and refined taste, has gradually transformed almost all England into a garden of beauty and delight — for in every part of this country industry is incessant, and hand in hand with industry goes thrift.

A vast gray tower rising superbly out of a dense mass of green and glistening foliage, a gray spire near at hand, visible amid a cluster of red and wrinkled roofs, and over all a flood of sunshine — and this is Ely! I had not been an hour in the town before I had climbed to the summit of the western tower of the cathedral, and gazed out upon the green and golden plains of Cambridgeshire, Suffolk, and Northampton, lit by the afternoon sun and blazing with light and colour for thirty miles around. Far to the

northwest you may just discern the black
tower of Peterborough. North and east,
at a still greater distance, a dim gray shape
reveals the ramparts of Norwich. Thirty
miles northward rise the spires of Lynn.
You cannot see them, but the wash of the
North sea breaks in music on that delicious
coast, and the strong ocean breeze, sweeping over the moors and fens, cools the
whole land and stirs its sun-lit foliage till
it seems to sparkle with joyous motion.
The Ouse [1] winds through the plain, at some
distance, south and east, — dark and shining in the glow of the autumn afternoon, —
while, gliding between hedges in the west
and south, come little railway trains from
Cambridge and Saint Ives. Nearer, far
below, and nestling around the great
church are the cosy dwellings of the clean
and quiet town — one of the neatest, most
orderly, most characteristic towns in Eng-

---

[1] This river, and not the Ouse that flows through
York, is Cowper's " Ouse, slow-winding through its
level plain." That poet's life (1731-1800) is associated with Berkhampstead, Hertfordshire, where
he was born; Huntingdon and Olney, in Bucking-
hamshire — both on the Ouse; Weston, in North-
amptonshire; and Dereham, in Norfolk, where he
died. His ashes rest in the parish church of Dereham.

land. Houses, streets, and trees commingle
in the picture, and you discern that the
streets are irregular and full of pleasing
curves, the buildings being mostly made
of light gray or tawny yellow brick, and
roofed with slate or with brown tiles that
the action of the weather has curiously
wrinkled and the damp has marked with
lichen and moss. At this dizzy height you
are looking down even upon that colossal
octagon tower, the famous lantern of Ely
(built by Prior Alan de Walsingham, a
little after 1322), which is one of the mar-
vels of ecclesiastical architecture throughout the world. It is a prospect at once of
extraordinary rural sweetness, religious
pomp, and august and solemn antiquity.
It is a pageant of superb modern civilisa-
tion and refinement, and yet, as you gaze
upon it, you forget all that is contemporary and present, and seem to be standing
among the phantom shapes and in the
haunted cloisters of the Middle Ages.

Each of the great abbeys of England has
its distinctive character. The beauty of
Ely is originality combined with magnificence. That cathedral is not only glorious;
it is also strange. The colossal porch, the
stupendous tower, the long nave with its

F

marvellous painted ceiling, the vast central
octagon, the uncommon size and the unusual position of the Lady chapel, the massive buttresses, the delicate yet robust
beauty of the flanking turrets, the wealth
of carved niches and pinnacles — all those
elements of splendour unite to dazzle the
vision and overwhelm the soul. Inside the
church there is nothing to obstruct your
view of it from end to end; the Gothic
architecture is not overladen, as in so many
other cathedrals in Europe, with inharmo-
nious Grecian monuments; and when you
are permitted to sit there, in the stillness,
with no sound of a human voice and no
purl of ecclesiastical prattle to call you
back to earth, you must indeed be hard to
impress if your thoughts are not centred
upon heaven. It is the little preacher in
his ridiculous vestments, it is man with his
vanity and folly, that humiliates the reverent pilgrim in such holy places as this, by
his insistent contrast of his own conventional littleness with all that is celestial in
the grandest architectural results of the
inspiration of genius. Alas, and again
Alas! When I remember what glorious
places have been almost ruined for me
by inveterate human gabble I know not

whether the sentiment that predominates is resentment or despair. But for every true worshipper the moment of solitude comes, and with it comes the benediction of beauty. During some part of last night I stood at my window, in the Lamb, and looked at the great cathedral, silent and sombre under the cold light of the stars. The wind was blowing, fresh and strong. The streets were deserted. The lights had been put out and the people had gone to rest. But it did not seem that the ancient church is a dead thing, or that slumber ever comes to it, or weakness, or forgetfulness, or repose. It keeps an eternal vigil, watchful over the earth and silently communing with heaven; and as I gazed upward at its fretted battlements I could almost see the wings of angels waving in the midnight air.

It is early morning now, and across a lovely blue sky float thin clouds of snowy fleece, while many rooks soar above the lofty towers of Ely, darting into crevices in its gray crown, or settling upon its parapets, with many a hoarse and querulous croak. The little town has not yet awakened. Nothing is stirring except a few dead leaves that the wind has blown down

over night, and that are now wildly whirled
along the white, hard, cleanly streets. The
level on which this ancient settlement
rests is so even and so extensive that
from almost any elevation you can see
the tree-line on the distant horizon. Some
of the houses have doors and shutters of
yellow oak. The narrow causeways are
paved with smooth gray stone or slate. Not
many lattices or gables are visible, such as
one sees so often in Canterbury and Winchester, nor is there in all Ely such a
romantic street as the exquisite Vicar's
Close, at Wells; but bits of old monastic
architecture are numerous, — arched gate-
ways fretted by time, shields of stone,
carved entablatures, and broken gargoyles,
— curiously commingled with the cottage
ornamentation of a more modern day. On
the long village-green in front of the cathedral stands a handsome piece of ordnance
that was captured at Sebastopol — peace-
ful enough now, before the temple of the
Prince of Peace. A little way off rises
the spire of St. Mary's, a gray relic of
the thirteenth century, remarkable for its
door-arches of blended Norman and early
English art. Close at hand is the venerable
Tudor palace, which for more than four

centuries has been inhabited by the bishops of Ely, and upon some part of which may have rested the gaze of that astute statesman, Bishop Morton, who "fled to Richmond," and whose defection wrought the political ruin of Richard III. Every way you turn and everywhere you ramble there is something to inspire historic memories or awaken impressive thought. Just as Glastonbury, upon the golden plain of Somerset, was once the Isle of Avalon, so this place, lonely among the fens of Eastern Anglia, was once the Isle of Ely. It is more than twelve hundred years since the resolute devotion of a chaste and noble woman made this a sacred spot; and if storied Ely taught no other lesson and gave no other comfort it would at least, — as the commemorative monument to the Saxon princess Ethelryth, — admonish us that life is capable of higher things than mortal love, and that the most celestial of women is the woman who is sufficient unto herself.

VIII.

FROM EDINBURGH TO INVERNESS.

INVERNESS, September 22, 1891. — The Pentland Hills vanish to the southward, under clouds of pale blue steel, through which the silver globe of the morning sun strives vainly to break its way, casting a dim gray twilight over the wide green landscape and adding to its beauty by fine contrast of colour.   The tide is out, as we cross the Forth bridge, and many boats are aground upon the sands beneath it; but many vessels, including a trim ship of war, are at anchor in the stream, and the graceful stone piers, the gray villages on the banks of Forth, and the miniature lighthouses on the little rocks along its channel make the same lovely picture as of old.   The water, much beaten by the equinoctial rain of the last two or three days, is smooth and of a sullen brown.   A cool wind is blowing, and birds are on the wing.   Soon the sunshine grows stronger and upon the emerald hills

and plains around Dunfermline there are
exquisite effects of golden light and passing
shadow. The old church-tower shows grand
beneath a wild sky, and in our fitful glimpse
of it we think of the grand life that it commemorates, and revere the good Queen
Margaret whose grave was made at its
base. On many hill-sides around this ancient city are sheaves of the harvest, and
we note the calm, self-absorbed cattle,
grazing in the wet meadows. The clouds
that had dispersed grow suddenly dense,
but shafts of sunlight linger continually on
the high summits of the bleak, distant hills,
and presently the blue of heaven shines
through great rifts in the sullen sky, and
all nature seems to be rejoicing after the
storm. The burnies, which are full to over-
flowing, rush gayly on their course and
murmur and sparkle as they speed. Scores
of sheep couch in the pastures, — the placid
images of innocent content. Loch Leven
is revealed to us, — its wide, gray water
gleaming in the fitful sun, — and as we
gaze upon its island and upon the little
dark town that is nestled on its shore, our
thoughts fly away to the remote days of
Mary Stuart, and we see her midnight flit-
ting across the stormy waves, and muse

once more upon the fascination of that imperial nature, victorious over so many noble souls, and now, at the distance of more than three centuries, still vital and still triumphant. Toward Perth the country grows more hilly and rocky, and we traverse tunnels and roll through deep ravines that are densely clad with the beautiful Scotch fir. Upon the more distant hills there are copses, which have an aristocratic effect of studied refinement, while numerous sheep, reposing amid the dark green broom, show upon the landscape like little balls of white wool. Down in the lowlands are haystacks shaped like ancient towers — one sign, among many others, of the manner in which the forms of the Middle Ages have affected the taste of to-day. Perth itself lies couched in a green glen, with lovely wooded hills around it, and as we enter its beautiful valley the sky is a dome of almost cloudless blue, flooded with golden light. Northward a brown-red castle rises stately among the trees, and soon we see the glistening water of the superb Tay winding through the most opulent meadows of Scotland. Never could memory lose such a picture, — the brilliant green of the fields ; the patches of red clover ; the beds of mari-

gold; the purple of heather; the wild luxuriance of the bracken; the vine-clad stone
walls; the groves of poplar, larch, oak, and
pine; the thick-leaved boughs tossing, and
the many-coloured flowers trembling, in a
cold, brisk wind; the constantly changing
outlines of the distant hills; and, over all,
the benediction of the golden sun. This
part of Scotland is as finely cultivated as
the best of England, and similar to it, —
and sometimes superior to it, — in effect of
opulence and beauty.

For a long distance after leaving Perth
our course is through a fertile valley. The
sun lies warm upon it and the vegetation is
very rich. No observer could fail to notice,
in that region, the splendid effect of sunshine glinting through the trees — the foliage
illuminated and glowing as if with internal
light. In a little while we come to Dunkeld,
and then presently to Dalguise. It is a
lonely country, — but all the lovelier for its
loneliness. The encircling hills are craggy
and gaunt rocks stare through the trees.
There is a wealth of woods, of remarkable
variety, and many pretty roads wind away
and are lost in them. The bushes are covered with hips and haws. The dark stream
of Tummel shines in a deep ravine. Pine

forests begin to crown the hills, and our gaze lingers pleased upon little shielings of gray stone, nestled in the sheltered dells. We are coming to Pitlochrie now, which is one of the loveliest places in the Highlands, and to that famous Pass of Killiecrankie, through which, in a frenzy of panic, the broken and bleeding ranks of the English fled from the victorious Highlanders of Dundee. The houses of Pitlochrie, made of gray stone and rising amid groves of birch and Scotch fir, are blazing with roses and with the brilliant purple shields of the clematis, and around them the crisp air is honeyed with the balmy fragrance of the pine. The Tummel and the Garry commingle here; the scenery blends rugged grandeur with tranquil refinement; and surely it may be said that few spots in Great Britain are lovelier than this one. A glowing autumn sun pours its flood of crystal light upon the wild Pass of Killiecrankie and the narrow rapid stream in the depth of the verdurous mountain gorge is burning with the lustre of a river of diamonds. Every element of great scenery, — excepting the American element of great size, — may be seen at Killiecrankie, and from there to Blair-Athole. They have marked with a memorial stone the place, upon the battle-

field, where the victorious Claverhouse fell,
— a mighty spirit ; a hero equally of history
and romance ; a great soldier ; perhaps, after
Montrose, the greatest soldier that Scotland
has ever known.   Our thoughts are full of
him as we rush through this wild and glorious region of his last battle, his brilliant
victory, and his triumphant death.   Ended
long ago was that unavailing strife — that
useless, pathetic waste of valour and vigour
and blood.   Nothing but an epitaph remains
to tell of it.   But genius can hallow whatever it touches ; and as long as the stars
hold their courses in the heavens this grand
mountain pass and haunted glen will keep
the hallowed memory of the great Marquis
of Dundee.   Scant pause is allowed for reverie.   The great are gone — but the sun
shines and the roses bloom, and if we would
see them at all we must see them now.
When Dundee fought his battle it was a
scene of wildness and of gloom.   It is a
scene of bloom and beauty to-day.   The
hills around Tummel and Garry are yellow
with hay-fields, and in the levels below there
are thick-fleeced sheep, and sleek cattle,
and graceful hayricks, and clumps of firs.
Blair-Athole sleeps in a vale of sunshine,
and around it, far away, rise the bold bare

peaks of the mountains that are Scotland's glory and pride. As the pageant lessens you see a vast range of wooded acclivity on the east and the river Tummel on the west, flowing at the base of brown and barren crags. Throughout this region the architecture of the gray stone houses is characteristic and superior; and if it lacks the repose of the English rural village it possesses a blending of solidity and piquancy all its own. The cone-pointed turret often rises among the trees, and the Tudor porch, covered with late roses, gleams forth from groves of fir; and everywhere there are shapes and objects of beauty — the rowan-tree, blooming and brilliant with its clusters of red berries; the blazing purple of the heather-clad hills; the fantastically figured groups of wandering sheep; the brown, transparent water of the rapid stream, — at intervals suddenly broken into a tumult of silver foam; and, far away, a faint, delicate, blue mist upon mountain peaks that seem to tower into heaven.

North of the Forest of Athole now — and our track is through a land of rock and heather, with not one tree to give it shade and with no creature stirring but an occasional sheep. For miles and miles we look

on nothing but lonely heath, extending up
the long mountain slopes on either hand,
desolate beneath the clear sunshine of a
September day. A solitary human being
is walking over the moor, and the dreary
waste grows drearier still, as our gaze rests
upon his dark figure and sees it fade away.
Soon we catch a momentary glimpse of
Loch Ericht, — the highest of the Scotch
lochs and reputed its gloomiest, — and grim
and gaunt enough it is, beneath the autum-
nal sky, which even now has begun to
lower with the remote approach of night.
Around us, at distance, the outline of the
hills is much broken, — range beyond range
of swart and grisly mountains rising upon
all sides and filling the prospect. We are
in the valley of the Spey and are traversing
the depth of Glen Truim. A backward
look through the hill-gap sees the whole
wild landscape under a semi-dome of silver.
Presently the glen becomes wooded; abodes
of man appear; hundreds of sheep are visible upon the moors; the mountain-peaks
are nearer and the mists creep down upon
them and swathe them in a silver fleece;
while a few birds (the first that we have
seen for hours) fly low in the glen. There
is a noble view of the Spey, whose broad,

black water, flowing beneath the three
arches of the bridge of Newtonmore, glis-
tens like ebony in the morning light. At
Kingussie we view a sumptuous fir-grove
and a ruined castle, and we are entranced
with the lovely effect of sunshine falling
here and there, from behind black clouds,
on hills that otherwise are lapt in shadow
and in mist. The landscape now is wonderfully various — a splendid breadth of
valley bordered with young firs and teeming
with dense foliage and with great masses
of purple heather. The village of Kincraig
is here — a gem to be remembered and
revisited — and sweet Loch Ellen is not
distant. We note the sharp and sudden
contrast of fir-groves with barren, desolate, rock-strewn hill-side. A lonely cabin
sweeps into view and a woman at the door
pensively looks at us as we pass. Loch
Inch is eastward from our track; Loch
Alvie westward. Yonder, upon a spur of
the mountain, is a monument to the Duke
of Gordon. There, to the northeast, rises
in a faint blue cloud the mysterious Cairn-
gorm mountain — which surely never looked
more beautiful than now. At Aviemore
the clouds lower and the mist is on the
hills, but in the sky behind them there is

a streak of silver. Miles of moorland succeed. The sky darkens. The wind is chill. The country is very lonely. If human beings are here they make but little sign of their presence. One low cabin we do indeed discern, — a mantle of green velvet moss upon its roof and many hens roosted on its window-sills in disconsolate meditation. The river Spey, broad and lovely, flows through this plain, and as far as the eye can reach its gaze lingers lovingly upon dense masses of dark green broom, among which, erect or couched, are the big and stately black cattle of the North. Fine gleams of sunshine fall suddenly, now and then, out of the gray sky, and rifts of wonderfully brilliant blue shine through the sombre rack of the storm. More and more we delight in the burnies that gleam like threads of silver on the hill-sides and bicker into foam and music as they come dashing through the plain. The clouds threaten but the landscape smiles. Near at hand is shadow, but far away the sunshine falls upon a yellow field amid the blue-green of the fir-trees and seems to make a glory over half the visible world.

It is the land of *Macbeth* through which we have been speeding, — "from Fife, great king," — and at many a place upon those desolate, rock-strewn moors of peat and heather the Shakespeare-lover has seen the "blasted heath," the storm-clouds hanging low, fantastic masses of mist drifting over the wet earth, Macbeth and Banquo with their marching forces, and the dim shapes of the three Weird Sisters gliding upon the haunted air. It was toward Forres that the victors were making, on that day of destiny when first the deadly purpose in the heart of Macbeth took form and voice in the evil angels who thenceforward were to lead him to his doom. We make toward Forres now. The sun, beneath dark clouds in the west, is sending down shafts of light upon a fertile valley, the harvest in sheaves, the yellow fields of oats, the cattle in pasture and the sheep in fold ; while the cold wind, sweeping over a woodland of birch and fir, is sweeter than honey. Forres next — a cleanly stone town with a cone-capped tower in the middle of it ; a place that is ample in population, active in enterprise, and abundantly possessed of the rewards of industry and thrift. At Brodie, looking across harvest fields and a low growth of firs, we see the glimmer of gray and leaden water and so

catch our first glimpse of the Moray Firth.
A little while, and we look upon the fine
gray spires of Nairn, and see the Moray
like a narrowing river, and beyond it the
bald, round mountains of Caithness, range
beyond range, disappearing in the angry
northern sky. Westward a narrow water-
fall of light, falling from a dense bank of
slate-coloured clouds, illumines a little
river, the garments that are bleaching on
the copious bushes of the broom, the level
lands of peat and heather, and the hard,
white roads that wind away toward Dal-
cross and Culloden. A mighty flock of sea-
mews momentarily darkens the air, and we
can hear their quick, sharp cries, and
almost the whirring rustle of their innumerable wings. The day is done, — a long and
lovely day of poetic pageant and unalloyed
delight, — and just as streaks of gold under
layers of blue and lead declare the sunset
we see the gray battlements and towers of
our desired haven, and glide to our rest in
the bosom of Inverness.

G

IX.

THE FIELD OF CULLODEN.

EASTWARD from Inverness, on the way to Culloden, the road at first skirts the southern shore of the Moray Firth, and the traveller driving on it sees a broad reach of shining water over which the sea-mews sport, and beyond it the bleak hills of Caithness, sleeping solitary in the sun. Soon the track bends southerly and then east again, and finally, passing beneath an arch of sumptuous beeches, it climbs the long hill-slope toward Drummossie Moor. The hedges on both its sides are filled with hips and haws and with the lovely blue-bells of Scotland, and from many a neighbouring glade of fir and birch sounds the clear, delicious call of the throstle, — turning the crisp air to music and filling the heart with grateful joy that this world should be so beautiful. Yonder on the hill is a massive gray tower, venerable with antiquity and stained as only time could stain it with the moss and lichen of age. Near at hand is the more humble dwelling of a cottager — decked with clematis and marigold. A single rook, poised upon the extreme topmost spike of a tall pine-tree, looks down upon the wide green fields, thick sewn with yellow flowers of the colt's-foot, and croaks with comfort. The warm sun is riding high in the cloudless blue of heaven and every wind is hushed. I could not have found a day of greater peace in which to gaze on a most desolate and pathetic scene of buried war. The first intimation that you receive of the battlefield is a gray rock at the roadside, directing attention to a couple of stone cottages in the adjacent field, — inscribed with the words, " King's stables: station of the English cavalry, after the battle of Culloden." The immediate approach to the centre of the field is made through a grove of pine-trees, with which Duncan Forbes, Laird of Culloden, — generously considerate of a cause to which his famous ancestor, Lord President Forbes, was inveterately hostile, — has caused it to be surrounded. You reach it almost before you are aware of its presence, and your heart must be hard indeed if you can look upon it without emotion. No spot that ever

I have seen so melts the soul with desolation and awe. I had been told that there
is but little at Culloden; and in the sense
of mere prose this may be true. There is a
large oval grassy plain, thickly strewn with
small stones. On one side of it there is a
lofty circular cairn. On the other side
there is an irregular line of low, rough
rocks, to mark the sepulchres of the clans
that died in this place, — brave victims of a
merciless massacre, heroic realities of loyal
love, vainly sacrificed for a dubious cause
and a weak leader. That is all. But to the
eyes of the spirit that lonely moorland, —
once populous with heroes, now filled with
their mouldering bones, — is forever hallowed and glorious with the pageant of
moral valour, the devotion and the grandeur
and the fearless fidelity of men who were
content to perish for what they loved. I
stood there a long time, in humble meditation. The faint white ghost of the half-
moon was visible in the western sky and
the place was so still that I could hear the
buzzing of flies in the air. No voice broke
the sacred silence, and from the neighbouring grove of pines no whisper floated —
though at a distance I could see their pendant tassels just swayed, and nothing more,

by the gentle autumn wind. Words have
their power; but it is not in the power of
any words of mine to paint the noble solemnity of that scene or to express the sublimity
of its spirit.

The battle of Culloden was an unequal
battle, and the issue of it seems to have
been for only a few moments in doubt.
The Highlanders — weakened by hunger
and want of sleep, wearied by a long and
useless night-march, and most unfit for
battle — were largely outnumbered. The
English artillery, strongly placed on a long
ridge of the moor, mowed them like stubble.
They swarmed from the hills on the west
and the south; but in the face of the English batteries their impetuosity was their
ruin. Their first charge did indeed break the
left wing of the first of the three English lines
that had been arrayed against them; and if
the Macdonalds had reinforced that charge
the final result might have been different;
but the Macdonalds had been denied the
place of honour, and they refused to lift a
hand. It is an old story now. The Duke
of Cumberland had commanded that no life
should be spared, and when the massacre
began men were shot down in droves. One
spot on the moor is marked "The Well of

the Dead." There the slaughter was fiercest
and bloodiest. The Chief of the Magillivray
fell there, and the rude lettering on that
rough rock commemorates one of the bravest
men that ever met a foe. No attempt has
been made at epitaph or mortuary recital·
Each rock of sepulchre bears simply the
name of the clan that was buried around
and beneath it, — Clan Fraser, Clan Mackin-
tosh, Clan Cameron, Clan Stuart of Alpin,
Clans Macgillivray, Maclean, and Maclach-
lan, and the Athole Highlanders, — those,
with the Mixed Clans, make up this roll of
honour, that neither change nor detraction
can tarnish nor time forget.

The Cairn of Culloden, erected in 1858,
suits the place as no other form of monument could suit it. Rugged truth and
homely simplicity are its characteristic attributes. It is a circular tower, about thirty
feet high and about ten feet in diameter.
It consists of twelve rows of heavy, irregular
stones, laid without mortar, but welded
with layers of slate. Upon the corner-
stone, at the south side, is sculptured the
commemorative record: "CULLODEN. 1746.
E. P. FECIT. 1858." The top is flat, and on
it is a wild growth of flowers and grass.
A tall slab, set at the base of its east front

and protected by an iron grill of pointed
shafts, bears this inscription :

THE BATTLE
OF CULLODEN
WAS FOUGHT ON THIS MOOR
16TH APRIL, 1746.
THE GRAVES OF THE
GALLANT HIGHLANDERS
WHO FOUGHT FOR
SCOTLAND AND PRINCE CHARLIE
ARE MARKED BY THE NAMES
OF THEIR CLANS.

Drummossie Moor extends for about six
miles along this region. It was vacant and
treeless in the wild days of the Pretender,
but in later times some of it has been cultivated and much of it has been reclaimed
and inclosed for pasture land. In a meadow
east of the cairn, called "The Field of the
English," are buried the soldiers of Cumberland who perished in that terrible fight.
Still further east, and at a point that commands a comprehensive, magnificent view
of the moor, the valley, and the southern
hills beyond it, stands a large, almost flat
rock, marking the position of the Duke of
Cumberland on the day of the battle — and
now inscribed with his execrated name.

Upon that rock you may climb, and as you
stand there and gaze over the green, heather-
spangled waste, — seeing no motion anywhere save of a wandering sheep or a drifting cloud, and hearing no sound except the
occasional cawing of a distant rook, — your
imagination will conjure up the scene of that
tremendous onset and awful carnage in
which the last hope of the Stuart was
broken and the star of his destiny went
down forever.   Here floated the royal
standard of England and here were ranged
her serried cohorts and her shining guns.
There, on the hill-slopes, flashed the banners of the Highland clans.   Everywhere
this placid moor — now brown and purple
in the slumberous autumn light — was brilliant with the scarlet and the tartan and
with the burnished steel of naked weapons
gleaming under the April sky.   Drums
rolled and trumpets blared and the boom
of cannon mingled in horrid discord with
the wild screech of bagpipes and the fierce
Highland yell ; and so the intrepid followers
of Royal Charlie rushed onward to their
death.   The world knows well enough now
— seeing what he became, and in what manner he lived and died — that he was un-
worthy of the love that followed him and of

the blood that was shed in his cause. The
student of politics may wisely instruct us
now that a victory at Culloden for the House
of Stuart might have meant the restoration
of the Roman Catholic church to its old su-
premacy over Great Britain, and thus might
have set back the kingdom to the iron
days of Henry VII. But when Culloden
was fought Charles Edward Stuart was
still, in Scottish minds, the gallant young
prince unjustly kept from his own, and the
clans of Scotland, never yet pledged to the
Union, were rallied around their rightful
king.   Both democracy and religion may
exult now, that the Duke of Cumberland
was the victor ; but, standing on that grave
of valour, with every · voice of romance
whispering at his heart, the sympathy of
the pilgrim is with the prince that was a
fugitive, the cause that was lost, and the
heroes who died for it — and died in vain.
I thought of Campbell's great poem of
Lochiel's Warning, — which first fired my
heart when I was a schoolboy, — and as I
recalled its full and fervid lines I was con-
firmed in the conviction that not in any language among men was there ever achieved
a more eloquent, passionate, sublime, and
therefore altogether poetic commemoration

of a great national event. To think of it
there was to place upon knowledge the crown
of inspiration ; and to have had the privilege of recalling it amid the scene which it
portrays will be a cause for gratitude as
long as I live.

NOTE. — The position occupied by Charles
Edward at the battle was under a tree, still
called Prince Charlie's Tree. Culloden House,
the manor of Lord President Forbes, stands a
mile north of the moor. On the top of the
Cumberland Rock I made the acquaintance of
H. H. Drake, LL.D., the venerable author of
the *History of the Hundred of Blackheath*,
who chanced to be sitting there. At Inverness
I spoke with Mr. Joseph Clegg, a bookseller,
who said he had known a very old inhabitant
who had pointed out, upon Drummossie Moor,
the exact burial-place of Keppoch, the gigantic chief of the Macdonalds, who fell while
vainly urging his discontented followers into
action. That spot the veteran remembered,
because, when a youth, it had been shown to
him by his father, a survivor of Culloden
fight : and persons digging there found the
bones of a very large man. The stones that
mark the sepulchres of the several clans were
erected by Duncan Forbes, Esq., in 1881.

X.

STORM-BOUND IN IONA.

IONA, IN THE HEBRIDES, September 30,
1891. — The wanderer who lands upon
the little stone ledge, partly natural and
partly artificial, that serves for a pier at
Iona should be prepared to remain upon
that island not simply as long as he likes
but as long as he must. In the Hebrides
the weather is the sovereign; and never
was there a sovereign more arbitrary, capricious, imperious, and potential. The poet
Longfellow, always felicitous in his choice
of epithets, never chose an adjective more
fitly than when he designated the western
islands of Scotland "the tempest-haunted
Hebrides."   At any moment the storm-
wind may sweep over them. At almost
any moment it may cease to blow. It seems
to know not any law except its own caprice.
When the tempest has spent its fury the
calm that reigns there is the calm of Para-
dise ; but while the tempest rages no sail

can brave the blast that beats those waters and no boat ever dreams of making for that perilous shore. The present pilgrim landed at Iona about noon on September 25, intending to return to Oban the next morning. Five days have passed, and there is but a faint prospect of his escape. Postal communication with the mainland — regularly occurrent but once every forty-eight hours in fair weather — has practically ceased. Telegraphic communication does not exist. If MacBrayne's steamer, the gallant and sturdy *Grenadier*, should come there will be a rescue. If not there must be a protracted exercise of the virtue of patience. Resting, however, in such a home-like haven as the St. Columba hotel, and cheered by companionship with the kind Highland hearts who dwell there, the practice of patience should not be difficult.

It was neither coarse weather nor fine when we sailed out of Oban. The sky was a dome of steel and the morning sun, beneath half-transparent clouds, was a disc of silver. At one point the sunrise splendour pierced its sullen veil and followed us with a diamond shaft of light. The wind was fresh; the sea lively; and now and

then there came a dash of rain. Northward we saw the ruined tower of Dunolly,
thick hung with ivy, and the black stone
upon the coast to which, as legend loves to
tell, King Fingal chained his dog. Far up
Loch Linnhe rose the huge back of Ben
Nevis, encumbered with sombre cloud.
More near, upon the right hand, glistened
the wet rocks of gray and lonely Lismore ;
while upon the left frowned the iron
shore of Mull. Upon the heights of Mull
shone the purple of heather and the rich
emerald of velvet turf. The lighthouse
tower upon Lismore stood out in bold relief against the sky, and over the furtive
rock where Maclean of Duart bound fair
Ellen of Lorn and left her to perish the
waves were breaking in wreaths of snowy
foam. All around were flights of sea-mews,
and we could see, in passing, upon the wide
ascending moors of Mull, the scattered gray
stone cottages and the cattle and sheep
sprinkled over the land. In the foreground
towered the iron-ribbed mountains of Morven, dark and terrible in their sterile solitude. The first time I ever saw Morven
the ghostly mists were trailing over its
sable parapets and there seemed no limit
to the altitude of its mysterious, inaccessi-

ble heights. This time its mountain masses
stood clearly disclosed in their grim grandeur
and cold, implacable disdain. The course
is northwestward between Morven and Mull,
and as we sped onward past the pleasant
town of Salen, secure in its little bay, the
clouds hung low, the waves glimmered
green in the fitful flashes of sunlight, the
sea-birds screamed their warning, and upon
both shores as far as the eye could reach
the white breakers foamed angrily against
dark, riven rocks. At most times I should
have seen those sights as signs of impending peril. I did not heed them then. There
are moments when the soul exults in storm
and danger — blindly feeling, perhaps, that
its fetters are momentarily broken and its
freedom at last begun. Besides, Scottish
scenery needs its environment of tempest.
You want no gentle breezes nor languorous
lights; but the frowning sky, the chill wind,
and the drifting mist.

Back of Tobermory, which is the capital
of Mull, there was sunshine on the distant
hills, and to our eyes, as we looked at it
from the sea, that ancient Highland town,
winding up its pleasant terraces on the side
of a noble cliff, seemed the chosen home of
adventure and romance. Ben More and

Ben Talla rose supreme at distance, bathed
in flying light; but Morven, under a slate-
coloured pall, was sullen and cold.   Soon
we discerned at our right the ruins of
Ardtornish, — where dwelt of old the Lords
of the Isles, and where the genius of Scott
has caused to be spoken that eloquent and
sublime blessing of the abbot upon royal
Bruce which is among the noblest strains
of poetry in our language.   Then, presently,
gaining the open sea, we looked all at once
upon the Tresnish Isles, — seeing Fladda
and Lunga and Black Mor, which is the
Dutchman's Cap, and Black Beg, and, far
to the southward, the misty outline of Iona;
while more to the north and west Tiree and
Coll, which are the haunted lands of Ossian,
lay like dim clouds on the horizon's verge.
Staffa is not seen as early as you see Iona
when steering this course, — which gradually turns southwest and south after Ard-
namurchan point is left to the northward, —
although it is nearer to you; for the other
isles of the Tresnish group partly hide it;
but it soon comes into view, lying upon the
lonely ocean like a long ship, dismasted
and at rest.   All the world knows that flat-
topped crag, covered with brilliant grass
and honeycombed with caverns in which

only cormorants and petrels breed and
haunt, while ocean listens to its own solemn
and tremendous music, whether of calm or
storm. We did not attempt to land, for the
sea had risen and the place was dangerous ;
but our boat steamed along the south side
of the island, and we gazed into Fingal's
Cave and into Mackinnon's and looked long
and wistfully at those mysterious basalt
columns which make a temple for the worship of nature, far grander than any creation of the hand of man. On a previous
occasion I had landed and explored the
caves ; and it is always wise, when any
form of experience has entirely filled and
satisfied the soul, not to attempt its repeti-
tion. The visitor to Staffa finds a sufficient
pathway, artfully contrived, along the face
of the cliff, and a rail by which to sustain
himself, so that he can enter Fingal's Cave
and walk nearly to the end of its cathedral
arch and gaze upward at its groined vault
of petrified pendant lava, and downward
into its black transparent depths where
only the monsters of ocean have their lair.
It is a solemn and awful place, and you
behold it without words and leave it in
silence ; but your backward look remains
long fixed upon it, and its living picture of

gloom and glory will never fade out of
your mind. We sailed away from Staffa
over a rough and angry sea — but no one
thought of it. The course is southerly, with
the great island of Mull upon the left hand,
Iona exactly ahead, and eighteen miles
distant in the solitary western ocean the
lighthouse on Skerryvore. We passed Loch-
na-Keal, which nearly divides Mull, and saw
at its mouth Gometra and Ulva, and, south
of them, Little Colonsay. It is to Ulva that
the hapless lovers would speed, in Campbell's
fine poem of *Lord Ullin's Daughter*. Gometra is the nearest land to Staffa, and it is
from Gometra that the boatmen row out,
in their life-boat, to carry visitors from the
steamer to the isle of caves, on days when
it is possible to land. Their boat was nowhere on the waters as we passed, and that
again should have been an omen; but I was
destined more and more to learn that the
fascination of Iona will not be baffled and
cannot be opposed.

Iona Sound is only one mile wide; but
it lies nearly north and south; the an-
chorage ground in it is uncertain and un-
safe; and, under the stress of a westerly
gale, the fierce waters of the Atlantic ocean
pour through it in one solid torrent of irre-

sistible force and fury. On both sides,
with but scant exception, the shore is
fringed with rock. On the Mull coast that
rock is generally a precipice. No splendour
of the horrible could exceed the horrid
grandeur of that iron shore — that grim and
terrible battlement which confronts and
defies the savage sea, from Kintra around
most part of the Ross of Mull. Toward the
southwest corner of Mull the Sound of
Erraid pours its tides into the Sound of
Iona, parting Erraid island from the larger
isle. The southwest corner of Erraid marks
the end of Iona Sound ; and not on all that
perilous coast is there any other spot so full
of peril. Here are the Torranen Rocks, —
the Otter, Frasiers, and the West Reef, —
and here, during days of almost unprece-
dented tempest, watching them for hours
and hours, have I seen great domes of
water, foaming upward fifty feet into the
air and gleaming perfectly black against the
livid sky. It was toward the time of sunset
on Friday (September 25) that the storm
finally broke upon us ; and from that moment onward, with but little pause, it has
continued to rage. Such a succession of
westerly gales has seldom been known
upon this coast. Such a glory of tempest

surely was never surpassed anywhere. All
the night of Friday the wind moaned and
howled around our little habitation, as with
the many threatening voices of hungry and
baffled beasts ; all night the rain was driven
in tumbling sheets against our windows ;
and all night I heard, in the darkness, the
long roar of the clamorous, resounding sea.
At morning, and at various other times during Saturday, there was sunshine, — fitfully
commingled with cloud and rain, — but at
no moment was there a lull in the gale ;
and when at noon I looked out upon the
Sound its great waves were rolling northward along its whole extent, in one regular
incessant procession of livid green ridges,
each reaching almost from shore to shore
and each mantled with an ermine crest.
No boat could have lived a moment in such
a sea. That night suddenly the wind fell,
the sky cleared, the air grew soft and
balmy, the stars came out innumerable and
glorious in the vast, dark vault of heaven,
and even the ocean curbed its anger and
changed its hollow roar to a soft and solemn
dirge. The sailors know this habit of the
gale and are not deceived by it ; the storm
has paused to catch its breath. Most of
Sunday that deceitful calm continued, and

no spot of earth ever looked more fair than lonely and beautiful Iona, — silent then, save for the sound of Sabbath bells mingled with the murmur of the many-coloured, musical sea. Late at evening, walking over the moors which are at the south of the island, I heard a sudden sharp note in the southern blast, and knew that a change was at hand. By midnight the wind was moaning in the chimney and whistling in shrill puffs through every cranny of the house, and as we lay awake in our anxious beds we could hear the swirl of rain, and from every quarter the horrid crash of breakers on the rocks. The morning of Monday dawned brightly, but it soon darkened, and all day long there was an alternation of shadow and sunshine, — now black clouds and sudden bursts of drenching rain, now a twilight of silver mist which sometimes turned to glittering rainbows over the stormy Sound, — but never was there a pause in the violence of the gale. In some hours of the ensuing night the moon cast her mantle of silver upon the raging waters, giving them a new beauty even in their wrath and menace. It is a long time, though, since I ceased to trust the moon, and I did not trust her then. The night-wind in the

chimney was a better monitor, and of that
night-wind in the chimney of Iona I shall
carry the memory to my dying day. Its
prophetic note was amply justified by the
continued storm of Tuesday — less violent,
perhaps, but not less effective. Often, that
day, did I climb upon Maclean's cross,
which stands on the causeway by the nunnery ruins, and there question the ocean,
now one way and now another, for the approach of any boat; but the colossal breakers on the Torranen rocks, seen though inau-
dible, were all my answer. That day, also,
climbing to the windy summit of Dun-i
(which is the highest mountain on this
island), I looked forth to the terrible crags
that gird its bay upon the west, and saw
Cabbach island, and Dite, and Musinal,
white with the flying shrouds of shattered
breakers, and the spouting cave in action,
hurling its snowy column far into the air,
to fall in a cataract of silver. It is a cruel
shore, look at it from what point you will.
Early this morning I was on the most placid
part of it that I have found, — the Martyrs'
Bay, — but even there the sullen waves
were storming up the beach and strewing
its hard white sands with long, serpent-
like grasses and with many sinister shapes

of the brown and wrinkled and slimy weeds
of the sea. To that beach, in ancient days,
came many a train of funeral barges, with
muffled banners and with coronach, bringing home dead kings of Scotland, for burial
in the Holy Isle. Over those white sands
was borne the mangled body of " the
gracious Duncan," who rests by Oran's
chapel, in yonder field ; and not long afterward, as many believe, was brought the
ravaged corse of his cruel murderer, to
sleep beside him in the same royal sepulchre. Duncan and Macbeth side by side,
and the grass growing over them, and the
wild sea-birds screaming above their nameless rest !

Such an opportunity for minute observation of this remarkable island is not likely
to occur again, and whether in storm or
calm, it has not been neglected. Standing
upon the summit of Dun-i the wanderer
looks northward to the hook-like point of
Iona and its wide curves of yellow beach
where the white breakers are sporting in
their dance of death. Mysterious Staffa,
in the northern distance, is distinctly visible. Eastward, across the swift and raging
channel, are the swarthy rocks of Mull,
with the treeless mountains of Mull and

Morven towering beyond them, blended in
one colossal heap of chaotic splendour.   In
the west is the wild Atlantic, breaking along
the whole three miles of crag and beach
that make Iona's outmost coast.   In the
foreground of the southern prospect is a
spine of rock-ribbed hill, beyond and around
which the land shelves downward into
levels, toward the encircling sea.   More
distant in the south the steeps once more
ascend, presenting a wide, broken surface
of lonely moorland, covered with rock and
heather, in which the shaggy black and
brown cattle, with their wide-spreading
horns and their great, luminous, beautiful
eyes, couch or stray, in indolent composure.
At the extreme southern point the isle presents a lofty crescent headland of riven
rock, — each cleft a dark ravine, and each
declining crag margined at its base with
cruel, jagged points, like iron teeth.   All
that savage scene, in one comprehensive
glance, the gazer from Dun-i may gather
into his vision ; and whether he regards it
as nature in her naked glory, or as the
holy ground that religion has hallowed with
her blessing and history has covered with
the garlands of deathless renown, he cannot
look upon it unmoved, and he can never

forget either its magnificent aspect or its
illustrious meaning.

Iona is three miles long, and at its widest
point a mile and a half wide, and it contains about two thousand acres of land, of
which about a quarter is under cultivation —
for oats, hay, vegetables, and flowers. Three-
quarters of it are devoted to pasture. There
are within its limits, of cattle, horses, sheep,
and other animals, about a thousand. The
collie dog and the household cat are frequently encountered, and you will not stroll
far upon the moors without meeting the
dark and stately Highland bull. I counted
about fifty dwellings. The population is
small. The minister of Iona, the Rev.
Archibald Macmillan, whose friendly acquaintance I had the pleasure and privilege
to gain, told me that his parish — which
comprises Iona and a section of the western
end of the Ross of Mull — contains about
five hundred and fifteen persons, of whom
about three hundred dwell in Mull. The
church is the Presbyterian church of Scotland, but there is also a free church. One
of the buildings is the manse. Another is
the schoolhouse. All the houses are made
of stone and some of them have a roof of
thatch which is held in its place by clamps,

superincumbent timbers, and heavy weights
of stone or iron. There are two hotels, —
one, the St. Columba, kept by Captain
Ritchie; the other, the Argyll Arms, kept
by John Macdonald — the official guide to
Iona, as his father was before him. The
crofters, all of whom are prosperous, live
in little stone cottages, rarely more than
one story high. The village consists of a
single street, with those humble huts ranged
upon one side of it — their doors and windows facing eastward toward the Sound.
The postoffice is also a shop, and there are
two or three shops beside. Three times
a week a little steamboat, sailing out of
Bunessan, — a town of Mull, sheltered in
Loch-na-Keal, — calls at Iona, if she can,
and takes away a mail, and leaves one, —
touching, by means of a skiff, at St. Ronan's
Bay. The settled part of Iona is a slope
upon its eastern shore, not distant from
the northern extremity — a region protected
by the hills from those westerly and southerly winds that are the scourge of the island.
There are only a few roads, but the pedes-
trian may readily make his way almost
anywhere, without fear of trespass. The
inhabitants are generally religious and are
orderly, courteous, and gentle. No doctor

dwells in the place and no resident of it is ever sick. Death may come by drowning or by other accident, but as a rule, the people live until they are worn out, and so expire, naturally, from extreme age. The Gaelic language, although it is dying away in the Highlands, is still spoken here. The minister, preaching on alternate Sundays at Iona and at Bunessan, speaks in English first, and then repeats his discourse in Gaelic, or he reverses that order, — and for both sermons he has an audience. It was my good fortune to hear him on September 27, together with about fifty other persons, seated on wooden benches in a whitewashed room, and I have never heard a preacher more devout, earnest, sincere, and simple. The school is largely followed, — the present attendance now being nearly seventy pupils, — and in the schoolhouse I found a library of nearly five hundred volumes (there are four hundred and fifteen titles in the catalogue), collected partly through the friendly ministrations of the Rev. Leigh Richmond, who visited Iona in 1820, and partly contributed by Mr. Thomas Cook, of London, the organizer of Cook's Tours. Shakespeare, Scott, Macaulay, Hume, Smollett, Tytler, Dickens, Sydney Smith, Cowper,

John Wilson, and J. R. Green, are among
the authors represented. Several volumes
of Cook's Voyages are there, and so are
ten volumes of Chambers' Encyclopædia.
Many sermons, however, appear in that
collection, together with many tomes of the
order of the everlasting Josephus — whom
everybody venerates and nobody reads.
Among the benefactors to the Iona Library
are the Rev. Dr. S. Dwyer; G. Gallie, of
Glasgow; A. Philp, of Bute; F. Clapp, of
Exeter; Rev. G. F. W. Munby, of Turvey;
Miss Copeland, of Dumfries; Miss Roberts;
and the directors of the Scottish Temper-
ance League. No newspaper is published
at Iona, but there is a little printing-office
near the St. Columba hotel, and from that
germ may be expected, one day or another,
such practical growth of enterprise and of
civilising thought as follows in the track of
a wisely ordered press. The Presbyterian
house of worship was built in 1830, and it
is a primitive sort of structure, now much
dilapidated; but in every attribute that
should appertain to the character of a
clergyman its minister would do honour to
the finest church in the kingdom. Iona is
owned by the Duke of Argyll, to whose
family it was granted by Charles I. Before

that time it had long been held by the
chieftains of the great house of Maclean.
When Dr. Johnson came here, with Boswell, in 1773, Maclean was their companion,
— then the lord of the clan, — and both
Johnson and Boswell have borne fervent
testimony to the unstinted hospitality with
which they were received, notwithstanding
that the Campbells were in possession of
the land. The sturdy doctor was obliged,
indeed, to sleep on the hay in a barn, with
his portmanteau for a pillow; but that was
the best accommodation attainable in the
island, and the Maclean slept beside him.
There is greater comfort to be found in
Iona now, but there is no luxury. Nor is
this a place for luxury. Here you are cut
off from the world. Here you are alone.
Here you are brought face to face with
eternity. Here, accordingly, if anywhere
on earth, the mind would be inspired, the
heart would be clean, and life would be
simple and pure. On one of those storm-
stricken days I stood alone upon the Hill
of Angels and looked off at the grim desolation of the dark Atlantic plain; and I
could not wonder, as I felt the overwhelming solitude and grandeur of the place, at
the old superstitious belief that when St.

Columba stood there, thirteen centuries
ago, the white-robed beings of another
world came floating down from heaven to
talk with their brother upon earth.

It is perhaps trite history that Columba
came from Ireland to Iona in the year 563,
bringing Christianity to the Picts of the
Western Islands, and that he made Iona
the fountain-head of religion and learning
for Northern Europe, — dying there A.D.
597, at the age of seventy-six. No one can
speak of Iona, though, without speaking of
her Saint. His spirit is indelibly stamped
upon the place, and whosoever walks in his
footsteps, must venerate his memory and
hallow his name. The monastic remains,
however, that the traveller finds in the
island are the ruins of red granite buildings
of a much later period than that of Columba
— structures that his pious labour had
rendered possible, but which his eyes never
beheld. The nunnery, St. Oran's chapel,
the cathedral and its adjacent fragments of
monastery, all roofless, and all the sport
of time and decay, are relics of about the
twelfth century. Parts of those ancient
fabrics are, possibly, of a date still earlier
— the noble cathedral tower (up which you
may ascend by a spiral stone staircase of

forty-two steps), the arches of its north
transept, and the simple form and massive
and beautiful arched doorway of St. Oran's
chapel bearing architectural traces of essentially remote antiquity. The church that
Columba erected did not stand upon the
site of the present cathedral ruin, but was
situated further to the north and nearer to
the sea; while the place of his cell — wherein
his pillow was the sacred heart-shaped stone
now preserved in the ruined chancel — is
believed to have been the site of a cottage
under the friendly shelter of Dun-i, a little
northward from the Argyll cross. (That
monument, picturesque in itself and melancholy in its loneliness, at the bleak roadside,
commemorates, " in the island that she
loved," that beautiful and lamented lady,
the first contemporary Duchess of Argyll.)
But whatever may be the measure of their
antiquity, those gaunt ecclesiastical relics
are more holy and beautiful than words
can tell, in their lone magnificence and desolate grandeur of ruin and decay. Accurate
detail of what they are and of what they
contain is well-nigh impossible, even to antiquarian research. The ravages equally
of barbarian hordes and of relentless time
have left scarcely anything in its place,

whether of statue, or carving, or inscription, or symbol, or brass, or picture, or memorial stone. But of their general character, — their rugged strength, their romantic aspect, their awful solemnity of isolation amid a wilderness of brown crag and tempestuous sea, — and of the sublimity which they must have derived as well from their sacred purpose as from their marvellous natural investiture, it is not difficult to judge. Imagination supplies every defect of knowledge, and the spirit that gazes upon those remnants of vanished greatness is lifted far above this world. The natural scene is the same to-day that it was of old. A thousand years make no change in those pitiless rocks and that stormy and savage clime. But man and all his works, — all his hopes and fears, his loves and hatreds, his ambitions and passions, his famous deeds, his labours and his sufferings, — have been swept away, and are become even as an echo, a shadow, a hollow, dying word, a pinch of dust borne seaward on the gale. In the precincts of the cathedral, there, at the foot of Oran's chapel, was the burial-ground of the kings of Scotland — Releig Oran. The grass grows thick upon it. No stone remains in its original place. The

rude letters and symbolic carvings have
been blasted by time and storm. The dust
of the humbler dead has mingled with the
dust of warriors and of princes in its royal
soil. The rooks that haunt the ruined
cathedral tower caw over it as they pass,
and over it sounds forever the melancholy
booming of the surges of the restless sea.
It is a place of utter desolation, where nothing reigns save nature's stony mockery of
all the achievements of man. What colossal forces of human strength and feeling
lie hushed and cold beneath that humble
sod ; what heroes of forgotten battles ; what
heroines of old romance ; what black, self-
tortured hearts of specious, ruthless mur-
derers ; what busy brains of crafty, scheming
statesmen, toiling ever through tortuous
courses for the power that they never could
long maintain ! Monarchs and warriors
that fought against Rome, in the great days
of Belisarius and Constantine ; kings that
fell in battle and kings that died by the
base hand of midnight murder ; kings that
perished by the wrath of their jealous wives,
and kings who died peacefully in the arms
of mother church ; princes of Ireland and
of Norway, and Lords of the Isles — there
they all sleep, in unknown graves and in-

accessible solitude, beneath the brooding wings of oblivion. Hard must be the heart, insensible the mind, that could dwell upon that stupendous scene of mortality without awe and reverence, or could turn away from it without having learned, once and forever, the great lesson of humility and submission.

NOTE ON MACBETH AND DUNCAN. — It is a part of the tradition that Macbeth, after his defeat on "high Dunsinane hill," which is about eight miles northeast of Perth, was overtaken in flight, and was slain, at Lumphanan, a little north of the Dee, about midway between Ballater and Aberdeen. A cairn that bears his name, and is dubiously said to mark his grave, may be seen in a meadow of Lumphanan. Authentic historians, however, declare that his remains were conveyed to Iona, which had been the imperial sepulchre from, at latest, the time of Kenneth III, 974. The custom was to embark the royal corse at Corpach, on Loch Eil. The funeral barges would thence make their way through lonely seas to the holy isle. The burial of Duncan at St. Columba's Cell is mentioned by Shakespeare:

> " *Rosse.* Where is Duncan's body?
>   *Macduff.* Carried to Colmes-kill,
> The sacred store-house of his predecessors
> And guardian of their bones."

I

II

SHRINES OF LITERATURE

XI

IN Shakespeare's youthful days the Forest
of Arden was close at his hand and
there is no doubt that he often wandered in
it and that he knew it well. It covered a
large tract of country in Warwickshire, extending from the west bank of the Avon
six or eight miles northwest of Stratford,
and while that region is cleared now, and
beautifully cultivated, and sprinkled with
trim villages and lovely manors, and diversified with many appellations, the general
name of Arden cleaves to it still. Many of
its great trees, indeed, sturdy and splendid
at a vast age, remain in flourishing luxuriance, to indicate what it was; and if you
stand upon the hill near Beaudesert church
— where once the banners of Peter de Mont-
fort floated from his battlements — and
gaze over the adjacent plains, your eyes
will rest upon one of the sweetest landscapes
in all the delicious realm that environs the

heart of England.   It is idle to suppose that
Shakespeare was unacquainted with that
old woodland and the storied places round
about it — with Wroxall Abbey, and the
moated grange of Baddesley Clinton, and
all the historic spots associated with the
wars of Henry III., the dark fate of Sir
Piers Gaveston the handsome Earl of Cornwall, and the romantic traditions of the
great house of Warwick.   From his earliest
boyhood this region must have been his pre-
empted field of exploration and adventure
and must have been haunted for him with
stately shapes and glorious visions.   His
mother's name was Mary Arden; and we
may be sure that with her name, to him so
beautiful and so sacred, he always associated the freedom and the splendour of
that romantic forest.   When therefore we
read his exquisite comedy of *As You Like
It*, and observe, as we cannot help observing, that every flower that blooms, every
leaf that trembles, and every breeze that
murmurs in it is redolent of his native
Warwickshire, we are naturally disinclined
to surround a purely ideal and fanciful
conception with the accessories of literal
France, or to endure an iron-bound conventionality of treatment in the illustration of it.

There are, to be sure, a few French names in the piece, and in its first scene Oliver designates Orlando as "the stubbornest young fellow of France"; but later we meet with the serpent and the lioness, indigenous to the jungles of Asia. The story upon which, to a considerable extent, it was founded — Thomas Lodge's novel of *Rosalynd* — is French in its location and its persons; but Shakespeare, in his use of that novel, has played havoc equally with the geography and the nomenclature. His scene is anywhere and nowhere; but if in this piece the wings of his imagination do brush against the solid ground at all it is against that haunted woodland of Arden which waved its sweet green boughs around his English home. *As You Like It* is an English pastoral comedy, through and through, and therefore it ought to be dressed in English pastoral robes — with such genial though discreet license as poetic fancy might prompt and approve — and it ought to be acted under such greenwood trees as bloom in the vale of the Red Horse, where Shakespeare lived and loved. Planché will have it — since Shakespeare has introduced possibly French dukes into the story, whereas in the original those potentates are cer-

tainly French kings — that the action must
be supposed to occur in France, and to occur at a time when yet independent duchies
existed in that country ; and that time he
declares must not be later than the reign of
Louis XII. (1498–1515), who married Anne
of Brittany and so incorporated into the
royal dominions the last existing fief to the
crown. It must be a French garb of the preceding reign, says that learned antiquarian
and rose of heraldry — the reign of Charles
VIII. (1470–1498) ; and that will be picturesque and appropriate. In that way at once
this lawless, lilting, drifting fiction is
brought within the precise lines of fact and
duly provided with a local habitation. A
distinct purpose and a definite plan, of
course, there must be, when a piece is to be
acted : only it should be urged and allowed
that in dealing with this exceptionally va-
grant play the imagination ought to be permitted to have a free rein. *As You Like It*
is a comedy which in a peculiar and unusual degree requires imagination ; and not
with those only who present it but with
those who see it performed.

The composition of this piece occurred at
a specially interesting period of Shakespeare's life. He was in his thirty-fifth

year, and he had, as it proved, lived two-thirds of his allotted time. He had written all but one (*Henry VIII.*) of his English historical plays; he had written eight out of his fourteen comedies; he had written *Romeo and Juliet;* while his great tragedies of *Hamlet* and *Julius Cæsar* were close at hand and must have been much in his thoughts. [The first draft of *Hamlet*, indeed, may have been written long before his thirty-fifth year.] Imagination had obtained full possession of him by this time, and he was looking at life with a comprehensive vision and writing about it with an imperial affluence of freedom, feeling, and power. No work of art was ever yet created by anybody without labour, but the proportion of effort differs in different cases, and surely no quality is more conspicuous in *As You Like It* than that of spontaneity. The piece is exceptional for its fluent grace. It must have been written easily and in a happy, dream-like, careless mood, half reverie and half frolic. There is much wise philosophy in it, veiled with playfulness; there is much in it of the poetry which with Shakespeare was incidental and natural; and here and there it is lightly touched with the pensive melancholy of a mind that is

disenchanted with the world: but its predominant tone is sprightly; and we may
be sure that Shakespeare was at ease in
its creation, and perhaps we may discern in it much of his temperament and
of his habitual mental attitude — which
apparently was that of calm, benign, humorous, half-pitying, half-playful tolerance
— toward human nature and human life.
He threw aside all restraint when writing this play, and allowed his fancies to
take care of themselves. The persons
who figure in *As You Like It* are all,
in some measure, shadowy. They are at
once real and unreal. They lay hold of
experience but their grasp is frail. The
loves of Orlando and Rosalind are not the
loves of Romeo and Juliet. The cynical
musings of Jaques are not the corrosive
reflections of Hamlet. The waggish drollery of Touchstone is not the pathetic levity
of the Fool in *Lear*. The drift, the substance, the significance is "as you like it"
— as you may please to find it; grave or
gay, according to the eyes with which you
look and the heart with which you feel.
Those persons, entangled with incidents
that are mostly impossible, flit about under
green leaves, amid the mossy trunks of

slumberous trees, in dells that are musical with bird-songs and running water and resonant with the echoes of the huntsman's horn; and while the fragrant wind blows on their faces and the wild deer dash away at their approach they play their parts in a sweetly fantastic story of fortune's vicissitudes and love's delays, such as never could literally have happened in the world, but which the great poet, in his own wonderful way, has made tributary to an exposition of the strongest contrasts that human experience can afford. There is one obvious lesson to be deduced from this understanding of the subject. The reader or the spectator who would fully enjoy *As You Like It* must accept it in the mood in which it was conceived. He knows that lions do not range French or English forests, and that Rosalind, though in man's apparel, would at once be recognised by the eyes of love. Yet to those and to all discrepancies he is blind. He even can assent to the spectacle of Jaques stretched beside the brawling stream at the foot of the antique oak, speaking his sermons upon human weakness, folly, and injustice, with nobody for an audience. He feels himself set free from the world of hard facts. He is in Arden.

The antiquated metrical story, Coke's *Tale of Gamelyn*, which is older than Chaucer, was the precursor of Lodge's novel of *Rosalynd*, or *Euphues' Golden Legacye*, published in 1590, and this novel of *Rosalynd*, by one of Shakespeare's contemporaries, was in turn the precursor of *As You Like It*. Shakespeare followed the novel in his use of incidents and conduct of plot, but he has transfigured it by his investiture of the characters with new and often exalted personality, and by his poetical expression and embellishment of them. He furthermore invented and introduced Jaques, Touchstone, and Audrey. The comedy was not printed during his lifetime and it did not make its appearance till Heminge and Condell published the first folio, in 1623. The piece as there given is divided into acts and scenes. The text was subsequently altered for the second folio (1632), and substantially according to the form then adopted the comedy has survived. The first text, however, is a good one. Those discrepancies, by the way, between the texts of the four Shakespeare folios, interfere sadly with the addle-headed and superfluous industry of Mr. Donnelly and his disciples in their manufacture of Bacon cryptograms. The first performance of *As You Like It* appears to have occurred at the Globe theatre in the first year of its existence (that house was opened early in 1599 and was burnt down on June 29, 1613), and an ancient and apparently authentic tradition (it was first recorded by William Oldys, 1687–1761) declares that Shakespeare himself acted in it as Adam. The epilogue is thought to be, at least in part, spurious. It obviously was written with a view to its being spoken by the boy who played the woman part of Rosalind in Shakespeare's time and later. It is a feeble composition, whoever wrote it. It is slightly altered for stage use.

It has often been urged that the necessity of providing occupation for a dramatic company and of furnishing a novelty to win the public attention and support is a sufficient motive, or impulse, or inspiration for the making of a good play; and the believers in that doctrine — that eminent Shakespeare scholar Richard Grant White being conspicuously one of them — usually point to Shakespeare as an example in proof of this practical and sordid theory. But Shakespeare's plays it is found, tax to the utmost limit the best powers of the best actors;

and furthermore those plays contain, as a
rule, more material, and that of a higher
order, than the average public has ever
comprehended or ever will comprehend. If
indeed Shakespeare wrote his plays simply
to fit the company engaged at the Globe
theatre and the Blackfriars — in both of
which he appears to have owned an interest
and at both of which the same company
performed — or if he wrote them simply to
please the passing caprice of the time, he
must have had a marvellous dramatic company in his view, and he must have been
aware of a still more marvellous community
to be addressed. Either this or assuredly
he made needless exertions, since he has
over-freighted his plays with every sort of
mental and spiritual wealth and beauty.
The affluence of mentality in the comedy of
As You Like It — consisting in the quaint
whimsicality of its humour, the complex
quality of its chief characters, the airy, delicate, evanescent poetry of its atmosphere,
the sequestration of its scene, and the fantastic caprice and indolent drift of its incidents — has always rendered it a difficult
play for actors to treat in a perfectly ade-
quate and successful manner, has always
kept it rather remote from general appreci-

ation, and has made it a cause of some perplexity to the critical mind. The truth
doubtless is that Shakespeare, out of the
necessities of his nature and not merely out
of those of worldly circumstance, while la-
bouring for the stage, wrote for a larger
theatre than ever was comprised within
four walls and in accordance — whether
consciously or not — with higher laws of
expression than those that govern a theatrical manager in the matter of demand and
supply in dealing with the public. He was
not a photographer ; he was an artist. He
did not copy life ; he transfigured it and
idealised it. The great creations of his
dramatic genius are not actual men and
women of the everyday world ; they are
representative types of human nature, and
there is always a deeper meaning in them
than the obvious one that appears upon the
surface. The same mystery invests them
that nature has diffused around the origin
and destiny of the human soul. For this
reason they inspire incessant interest, and
hence it is that the field of Shakespearean
study can never be exhausted.

In *As You Like It* Shakespeare's mood,
while happy and frolicsome, is also whimsical, satirical, full of banter, covertly wise

but outwardly fantastic. He fools you to the top of your bent. He is willing that you should take the play in earnest if you like to do so, but he smiles all the while at your credulity. He will end it rationally enough, in the matter of doing poetic justice; but in the meanwhile he has turned everything upside down and he is making merry over the spectacle. Such incidents as the radical conversion of the wicked duke by the good hermit and the instantaneous regeneration of the malignant Oliver by his brother's single act of generosity are sufficiently typical of this poetic pleasantry. The most sonorous and apparently the most searching observations upon human experience are put into the mouth of Jaques; but Jaques is perhaps the least sane and substantial of the representative persons in the comedy — being an epicurean in sentiment and a wayward cynic, whose remarks, although quite true as far as they go and wonderfully felicitous in manner, really contain no deep truth and no final wisdom, but are alike fragile and fantastic; as any one can see who will, for a test, set them beside either of the four great soliloquies in *Hamlet*, or beside the principal speeches of Ulysses, in *Troilus and Cressida*. The wisest

man in the play is the professed Fool, — by
whom and by the old servant Adam the
only manifestations are made that the piece
contains of the highest of human virtues,
self-sacrifice : for even as Adam devotes all
to Orlando so does Touchstone devote all
to Celia.   No especial stress was laid on
the lover.   He is handsome, pure, ingenu-
ous, and brave, and he serves his purpose ;
but it is evident that Shakespeare loved
Rosalind, since in drawing her he ceases to
jest.   Rosalind is not merely the heroine of
an impossible courtship in a visionary forest ; she is the typical perfection of enchanting womanhood.   She is everything that
man loves in woman.   She is neither an
angel nor a fairy.   She is flesh and blood ;
and while her mind and accomplishments
are noble and her attributes of character
poetical, she is depicted in absolute har-
mony with that significant line, wrapping
truth with a jest, in Shakespeare's one hundred and thirtieth sonnet,

" My mistress, when she walks, treads on the
      ground."

Amid the sprightly caprice, the tantalising
banter, the drift and whirl of fantastic incidents, and the glancing lights of folly and

K

wisdom that constitute this comedy the
luxuriant, sumptuous, dazzling, entrancing
figure of Rosalind stands out clear and firm
in the warm light of its own surpassing
loveliness. And this is the personality that
has from time to time brought *As You Like
It* upon the stage, and temporarily at least
has kept it there.

At the time of Shakespeare's death (1616)
two movements had already begun which,
gathering power and momentum as the
years rolled on, have done much to shape
the dubious, shifting, political condition of
the world of to-day. One of these was a
movement in favour of government by the
many; the other was a movement against
the Roman Catholic church. Both prevailed in the establishment of the Common-
wealth, and one of the first institutions that
went down under them was the British
Drama. Shakespeare was an exceedingly
popular author during his lifetime, and his
works must have been in request for a considerable time after his death, because the
first folio, 1623, was succeeded by another
in 1632; but soon after that date theatres
and plays began to drop out of the public view. The fecundity of play-writers
between Shakespeare's theatrical advent

(1588) and the year 1640 must indeed have been abundant, since out of nearly or quite six hundred plays that got into print in England before the Restoration (1660) only fifty-eight are thought to have existed before Shakespeare began to write. The others, therefore, must have been made during and after his immediate time. But the war between Charles I. and his Parliament put an end to that dramatic episode; and presently, when the Puritans prevailed, they authorised by law (1647) the destruction of theatres and the public flagellation of actors. There is a great darkness, of course, over that period of theatrical history. Soon after the Restoration, indeed, the third folio of Shakespeare's works made its appearance (1663–64), containing six if not seven plays that were spurious; and in 1685 came the fourth folio; yet all the while Shakespeare seems to have been banished from the stage, and in general from contemporary knowledge. Dryden mangled his lovely comedy of *The Tempest* (1670), and his noble tragedy of *Antony and Cleopatra* (1678), and sapiently referred to his manner as "out of date." Not till the period of Queen Anne did the Shakespeare revival begin, and even then it was a languid force.

But it began — and little by little the plays
of the great master made their way back to
their rightful pre-eminence.

As You Like It, after its first career at
the Globe theatre — and whether this was
long or short nobody knows — seems to
have sunk into abeyance and to have remained unused for a long time. It may
have been revived at the period of the Restoration, but I have found no record of its
presentation in that epoch. An injurious
alteration of it, called *Love In a Forest*, by
Charles Johnson, was acted at Drury Lane,
for six nights, in 1723, and was published
in that year; but it is the opinion of Genest
that the original piece was not acted in
England at any time after the Restoration
until 1740. On December 20 in that year
it was brought forward at Drury Lane with
a brilliant cast. Mrs. Pritchard was the
Rosalind. This was repeated on January
16, 1741, and twenty-five times during that
season. Within the next sixty years *As
You Like It* was reproduced upon the London stage thirteen times.

The immediate competitors and the successors of Mrs. Pritchard as Rosalind,
counting to the end of the eighteenth century, were Peg Woffington; Mrs. Dancer

(who subsequently became Mrs. Barry, wife of Spranger Barry, and finally Mrs. Crawford); Mrs. Bulkeley; Miss Younge; Miss Frodsham; Mrs. Siddons; and Mrs. Jordan. Peg Woffington as Rosalind delighted everybody. Her first performance of the part was given during her first season on the London stage, after she had left Covent Garden and gone to Drury Lane, where she first appeared on September 8, 1741, as Sylvia in *The Recruiting Officer*, under the management of Fleetwood. Kitty Clive played Celia when Woffington first embodied Rosalind, and Theophilus Cibber played Jaques. It was in Rosalind that this great actress was last seen upon the stage, May 3, 1757, in Covent Garden — the tragic fact of her collapse while speaking the epilogue being one of the best known incidents in dramatic history. Without doubt she was the best Rosalind of the eighteenth century. Mrs. Dancer came next and was deemed superb. Mrs. Siddons first acted the part on April 30, 1785; but as might have been foreseen she did not succeed in it. The record made by Genest is explanatory and explicit: "Mrs. Siddons contrived a dress for Rosalind which was neither male nor female. For this she was

ridiculed in the papers, and very deservedly.
She had it entirely at her option to act
Rosalind or not to act Rosalind ; but when
she determined to act the part it was her
duty to dress it properly. Mrs. Siddons
did not add to her reputation by her performance of Rosalind, and when Mrs. Jordan had played the character few persons
wished to see Mrs. Siddons in it." Mrs.
Abington, in a conversation with the veteran Crabb Robinson, mentioned that effort
on the part of Mrs. Siddons long afterward
(June 16, 1811). "Early in life," she
remarked, "Mrs. Siddons was anxious to
succeed in comedy, and played Rosalind
before I retired." And Mr. Robinson in-
genuously adds : "Mrs. Siddons she praised,
though not with the warmth of a genuine
admirer." Mrs. Jordan first acted Rosalind on April 13, 1787. This was also at
Drury Lane. John Philip Kemble played
Orlando. The success of the actress was
brilliant. It was felt that the part had not
been acted in such a winning manner since
the days of the incomparable Woffington.
"The elastic step, the artless action, the
sincere laugh, and the juicy tones of her
clear and melodious voice" (John Galt)
were all, we may be sure, delightful embel-

lishments of that performance. "Her Rosalind," says Oxberry, "was exquisite." Mrs. Jordan herself, however, seems to have taken a different view of the subject, since long afterward, in the green-room at Covent Garden on a night when she was playing Rosalind, she said to John Taylor (*Records of My Life*, p. 122): "If the public had any taste how could they bear me in the part which I play to-night, and which is far above my habits and pretensions!" Of Mrs. Dancer as Rosalind (1767), the same memoir makes enthusiastic mention no less than three times in different chapters. "Mrs. Dancer's Rosalind," says that veteran judge, "was the most perfect representation of the character that I ever witnessed. It was tender, animated, and playful to the highest degree. She gave the 'Cuckoo Song' with admirable humour."

Since 1800 *As You Like It* has been often in the public view on both sides of the Atlantic. Its first revival at London within the present century was made on October 25, 1805, at Covent Garden. The cast then included John Philip Kemble as Jaques, Charles Kemble as Orlando, Fawcett as Touchstone, Incledon as Amiens, Murray as Adam, Brunton as Oliver, Blanchard as

William, Miss Smith as Rosalind, Miss
Brunton as Celia, and Mrs. Mattocks as
Audrey. The book of this play, as revised
and prepared for the stage by J. P. Kemble,
was published in 1810. Macready on various occasions enacted Jaques, but he has
left no record of it that is usefully significant. His first performance of it was given
in 1819-20, at Covent Garden. "Jaques
was a study for me," he says, in his *Auto-
biography*, "one of those real varieties of
mind with which it is a pleasure in representation to identify one's self." Samuel Phelps,
however, who participated in Macready's revival of the comedy at Drury Lane on October 1, 1842, told his biographer John Coleman
that it was "the most superb production of
As You Like It the world has ever seen or
ever will see." Rosalind was then taken by
Mrs. Nisbett. "Not having seen her," said
the veteran, "you don't know what beauty is.
Her voice was liquid music. Her laugh—
there never was such a laugh ! Her eyes,
living crystals, lamps lit with light divine !
Her gorgeous neck and shoulders — her
superbly symmetrical limbs, her grace, her
taste, her nameless but irresistible charm.
. . . You may rave about Helen Faucit's
Rosalind, but you never saw Nisbett."

This estimate, so much in the vein of Sir Anthony Absolute's description of Lydia Languish, glances at a woman whose portraits show her to have been very beautiful. She was the daughter of Captain Macnamara, who is supposed to have suggested the immortal Costigan, and she is said to have been the original of Miss Fotheringay, in *Pendennis*.   Macready's comment on that revival of *As You Like It* is in humorous contrast with that of Phelps. "The only shortcoming in the whole performance," he said to Lady Pollock, "was the Rosalind of Mrs. Nisbett, a charming actress in many characters, but not equal to that. She was not disagreeable, but she was inadequate."   And Macready spoke of having introduced into his revival, with excellent effect, the delicate tinkle of sheep-bells, as if the flock were somewhere feeding in pastures incident to the Forest of Arden.   The best of the Rosalinds in his eyes, and indeed in the eyes of many judges of a past generation, was Helen Faucit, now Lady Martin, who acted the part for the first time on March 18, 1839, at Covent Garden, with James Anderson as Orlando, Macready as Jaques, and Phelps as the First Lord.   Ellen Tree (Mrs. Charles

Kean) came next, who acted Rosalind on September 13, 1839, at the London Haymarket, and the old records abound with praises of her performance. Buckstone appeared as Touchstone, Phelps as Jaques, and Priscilla Horton (Mrs. German Reed), as Celia. Several English actresses have assumed Rosalind since the time of Ellen Tree — but only one has eclipsed her, the late Adelaide Neilson, who was superbly beautiful in the part and a vision of dazzling glee. Fanny Kemble has often given readings of *As You Like It*, but she has not acted in it.

On the British stage Rosalind has been played also by Fanny Cooper (Mrs. T. H. Lacy), who had the aid of G. V. Brooke as Orlando ; Isabella Glyn (Mrs. E. S. Dallas); Millicent Palmer ; Jane Elizabeth Vezin (Mrs. Charles Young) ; Carlotta Leclercq (Mrs. John Nelson) ; Mrs. Rousby ; Mrs. Scott-Siddons ; Mary Provost (Mrs. Samuel Colville), at the Princess's, London, July 9, 1861 ; Julia Bennett (Mrs. Barrow) ; Amy Sedgewick (Mrs. Goostry) ; Madge Robertson Kendal (Mrs. W. H. Grimston) ; Miss Marriott ; Jean Davenport (Mrs. Lander); Mrs. Langtry ; Miss Marie Litton, and Miss Calhoun. At the Shakespeare Memorial theatre, and for the benefit of that institution, at Stratford-upon-Avon, Mary Anderson enacted Rosalind, for the first time in her life, on August 29, 1885, and afterwards she repeated the performance in various cities of Great Britain and the United States.

On the American stage *As You Like It* was acted on July 14, 1786, at the John street theatre, New York, with Mrs. Kenna as Rosalind. Ireland records this, together with other presentations of the comedy in New York prior to 1860. On June 21, 1796 it was performed at the John street theatre, with Mrs. Johnson as Rosalind, Mr. Hodgkinson as Jaques, Mr. Hallam as Touchstone, Mr. Cleveland as Orlando, Mrs. Cleveland as Celia, and Mrs. Brett as Audrey. Mr. Jefferson, grandfather of the Jefferson of to-day, enacted Le Beau. The famous Park theatre was opened with *As You Like It*, on Monday, January 29, 1798. The piece was acted only once, however, and the next mention of it that occurs in the story of the New York stage records its production on January 8, 1850, at the Astor Place opera house, where it was acted for the benefit of the American Dramatic Fund Association, with Charlotte Cushman as Rosalind, Burton as

Touchstone, Hamblin as Jaques, H. Bland
as Orlando, Chippendale as Adam, Mrs.
Abbott as Celia, Mrs. J. Gilbert as Audrey, and George Jordan as Le Beau.
The elder Wallack closed his first season at the old Broadway and Broome
Street house with seven performances of
As You Like It, ending June 13, 1853,
himself playing Jaques, with Laura Keene
as Rosalind, Mrs. Brougham as Audrey,
Lester Wallack as Orlando, Charles Wal-
cot as Touchstone, and Blake as Adam.
At Burton's theatre, which ultimately became the Winter Garden, this comedy was
represented on January 29, 1857, for the
benefit of Julia Bennett Barrow, a brilliant actress in her time, who embodied
Rosalind and who was a ripe and dashing
beauty in those days.   Burton enacted
Touchstone on that occasion, Charles Fisher
was Jaques, and Orlando was performed by
Mr. Belton — an earnest and picturesque
actor, now forgotten.   Laura Keene chose
Rosalind for her first character, when she
opened her theatre at 622 Broadway, on
November 18, 1856, and the cast then included George Jordan as Orlando, Charles
Wheatleigh as Touchstone, Dickinson as
Jaques, Burnett as Adam, Wemyss as the

Duke in exile, J. H. Stoddart as Corin, and Mrs. Grattan as Audrey.

On the American stage *As You Like It* was acted more frequently within the thirty years from 1860 to 1890 than it was on either side of the Atlantic during the preceding sixty years of this century. Several fine casts of its characters might be cited. On November 29, 1870 it was acted at Niblo's theatre, New York, with the best Orlando of the age, Walter Montgomery; and the cast then included E. L. Davenport as Jaques, Mark Smith as Adam, Mrs. Scott-Siddons as Rosalind, Vining Bowers as Touchstone, James Dunn as Amiens, and Milnes Levick as Duke Frederick. On May 2, 1871 a performance of it was given at Niblo's with E. L. Davenport as Jaques, and C. R. Thorne, Jr., as Orlando. Carlotta Leclercq played Rosalind, for the first time in New York, at Booth's theatre, on March 25, 1872. The Jaques was D. W. Waller; the Touchstone Robert Pateman. Adelaide Neilson played Rosalind, for the first time in America, on December 2, 1872, at Booth's theatre. J. W. Wallack, Jr., was Jaques. Fanny Davenport appeared at Booth's theatre on December 22, 1877 as Rosalind, with Charles Fisher as

Jaques. Ada Cavendish, who came to America in 1878, had not acted Rosalind on the English stage, but she assumed the part here and was admired in it. Rose Coghlan appeared for the first time as Rosalind on September 30, 1880, at Wallack's theatre. Mrs. Langtry's advent in this part was seen at the same theatre on November 13, 1882. Helena Modjeska assumed it on December 11, 1882, at Booth's theatre. A performance of *As You Like It* was given in the open air in the grounds of the Masconomo House, at Manchester, Massachusetts, on August 8, 1887, with Rose Coghlan as Rosalind, Osmond Tearle as Orlando, Frank Mayo as Jaques, Agnes Booth as Audrey, and Stuart Robson as Touchstone. This experiment had previously been made in England and had met with social favour.

Under the management of Augustin Daly by whom it was revived with scrupulous care and profuse liberality, to signalise the assumption of Rosalind by Ada Rehan, December, 17, 1889, *As You Like It* has been presented at various times and places. Mr. Daly's first season as a theatrical manager began on August 16, 1869, when he opened the Fifth avenue theatre in Twenty-fourth street. That season continued until July 9, 1870, and in the course of it he presented twenty-five plays, three of which were comedies by Shakespeare — *Twelfth Night, As You Like It,* and *Much Ado About Nothing.* Mr. Daly's dramatic company at that time consisted of thirty-three members, including E. L. Davenport, George Holland, William Davidge, James Lewis, George Clarke, D. H. Harkins, Mrs. Gilbert, Fanny Davenport, Agnes Ethel, Clara Jennings, Lina Edwin, Mrs. Chanfrau, and Mrs. Marie Wilkins. For the Shakespeare revival Mrs. Scott-Siddons, an actress then in the fresh enjoyment of public attention, was engaged as a star. Mrs. Scott-Siddons played Rosalind, and so did Mrs. Clara Jennings. The name of the former had for two years been prominently associated with the part. Mrs. Scott-Siddons made her first appearance on the London stage on April 8, 1867, at the Haymarket theatre, as Rosalind. Her first display of the character in America was made in a reading that she gave in New York, on October 26, 1868, in Steinway hall. She first acted the part in this country on November 14, at the Boston Museum, and her first representation of it in New York was given

on November 30, 1868, at the New York
theatre, under the management of Augustin
Daly. Her star was eclipsed by that of
Adelaide Neilson, who in her day held
Rosalind against all competitors. Ellen
Terry has often been urged to impersonate
Rosalind, but has declined to undertake it.

Shakespeare appreciated the value of
music in association with drama. There
are songs in *Hamlet, Othello, King Lear,*
and *Antony and Cleopatra.* There are
passages in *Macbeth* that obviously were
designed to be chanted. There is need of
music in the ghost scene in *Julius Cæsar*
and in the masquerade scene in *Romeo and
Juliet.* There is use of song in *King Henry
IV.* and in *King Henry VIII.* The comedies abound with music. *The Tempest* and
A Midsummer Night's Dream are exceptionally rich in strains that must be sung;
and songs also occur in *The Two Gentlemen
of Verona, The Merry Wives of Windsor,
All's Well That Ends Well, Much Ado
About Nothing, Love's Labour's Lost, Measure for Measure, The Merchant of Venice, A
Winter's Tale, Cymbeline, Twelfth Night,*
and *As You Like It.* Music has been affili-
ated with other plays of Shakespeare, but
with these it was associated by his own

hand. In *As You Like It* the songs are
" Under the Greenwood Tree " (Act ii.,
sc. 5) ; " Blow, blow, thou winter wind "
(Act ii., sc. 7) ; " What shall he have that
killed the Deer ? " (Act iv., sc. 2) ; " It was
a lover and his lass " (Act v., sc. 3) ; and
the verses allotted to Hymen (Act v., sc. 4),
" Then is there mirth in heaven," and
" Wedding is great Juno's crown." The
songs of Hymen, together with all that relates to that personage, are usually omitted
in the representation of this comedy. On
the other hand, the song that is sung by
Spring, commonly called the Cuckoo Song,
in *Love's Labour's Lost* (Act v., sc. 2),
" When daisies pied and violets blue," was
long ago introduced into *As You Like It*,
and for many years of stage usage it was
put into the mouth of Rosalind, immediately after the words " O, that woman that
cannot make her fault her husband's occasion, let her never nurse her child herself,
for she will breed it like a fool." The purpose of that introduction is obscure. The
effect of it has ever been to smirch the radiant, gleeful ingenuousness and piquant
banter of the happy-hearted Rosalind with
a suggested taint of conscious coarseness.
The Cuckoo Song, sprightly and felicitous

in itself, was set to exceedingly beautiful music by Dr. Arne (1710–1778), and it appears to have been first introduced into *As You Like It* in 1747, at Drury Lane, to have been allotted to Celia, and to have been sung by Kitty Clive.   At Covent Garden in 1775 Mrs. Mattocks sang it, and Mrs. Mattocks played not Rosalind but Celia.   The first Rosalind that ever sang it was Mrs. Dancer, at Drury Lane, in 1767.   The airs for the Greenwood Tree and the Winter Wind were written by Dr. Arne ; that of the Deer Song was written by Sir Henry Bishop.   It was a Lover and his Lass (sung by the Second Page in the original) and the verses of Hymen were set to exquisite melodies by William Linley, and these were retained in Daly's arrangement of the piece.   The Pages were kept in, and the droll episode of their singing to Touchstone was allowed to have its rightful effect in displaying still further the quaintness of that wise, facetious, lovable character.   Altogether the lovely comedy was presented substantially as Shakespeare wrote it — in the glad light of early springtime and in one continuous picture of sylvan beauty.

XII.

FAIRY LAND: A MIDSUMMER NIGHT'S DREAM.

BECAUSE Shakespeare, who lived only fifty-two years, wrote so much within that brief period, and furthermore because he wrote with such transcendent genius and ability, it has pleased theoretical and visionary observers to declare that he never wrote at all. Shakespeare viewed alone, they maintain, is a miracle, and therefore an impossibility; but Shakespeare and Francis Bacon, rolled into one, constitute a being who is entirely natural and authentic. The works of Shakespeare and the works of Bacon present, indeed, almost every possible point of dissimilarity, and no point of resemblance. The man behind Shakespeare's plays and poems and the man behind Bacon's essays and philosophy are absolutely distinct from one another and as far apart as the poles. The direct and positive testimony of Shakespeare's friend

and professional associate, Ben Jonson — a
close observer, a stern critic, a truth-teller,
a moralist, not over-amiable in his commentary upon human nature, and neither
prone to error nor liable to credulity — tells
the world, not only that Shakespeare wrote,
but in what manner he wrote. The assumption, implied in the Bacon theory, that a
poet capable of writing *Hamlet, Macbeth,
Lear,* and *Othello* either would or could, for
any reason whatever, wish to escape the
imputation of their authorship, is obviously
absurd. The idea that Shakespeare, hired
by Bacon to father those plays, could for a
period of years go in and out among the
actors and the authors of his time, and so
impose upon their sagacity and elude their
jealous scrutiny as to keep the secret of this
gigantic fraud, is simply ludicrous. The
notion that the man who wrote Shakespeare's poems — and those, admittedly,
were the work of William Shakespeare —
was the kind of man to lend himself to any
scheme of imposture is repudiated by every
intimation of character that those poems
contain; and the same may rightfully be
said of the man who wrote Shakespeare's
plays. The fact that the plays, which these
theorists would deny to Shakespeare's pen,

are entirely, absolutely, and incontestably
kindred with the poems, which they cannot
deny to it, stands forth as clear as the day-
light. The associate fact that the plays
contain precisely such errors as would naturally be made by the untutored Shakespeare, but could not possibly be made by
the thoroughly taught and erudite Bacon,
is likewise distinctly visible. Yet, all the
same — because Shakespeare, like Burns,
sprung from a family in humble station,
and was but poorly schooled — this prepos-
terous doctrine persistently rears its foolish
head, and insults with idle chatter the
Shakespearean scholarship of the world. A
prominent representative dramatist, Dion
Boucicault, had the astounding folly to
announce an hypothesis — apparently intended to be taken in earnest — that Shakespeare's *Hamlet* was written by Jonson,
Webster, Dekker, and Alleyne, in conjunc-
tion with Shakespeare, and under his super-
vision; a doctrine which, to any student
acquainted with those writers and their
times, is deplorably idle. For if there
be in literature any work which, from the
first line to the last, and in every word
and syllable of it, bears the authentic
pressure of one creative and predominant

mind — the broad-headed arrow of imperial dominion — that work is *Hamlet*.
Shakespeare's style, once known, can never
be mistaken. No man of his time, with the
single exception of John Fletcher, could
write in anything like his peculiar strain of
simplicity and power. In some of the historical plays there are traces of collaboration — as all readers know; but in his
greater plays the only hand that is visible
is the hand of Shakespeare.

This is especially true of *A Midsummer
Night's Dream,* and probably no better
mental exercise than the analysis of the
style and spirit and component elements of
that piece could be devised for those persons — if any such there be — who incline
to entertain either the Bacon theory or the
collaboration theory of the authorship of
Shakespeare. Bacon, if his avowed writings may be taken as the denotement of
his mind, could no more have written that
play than he could have flown on wings of
paper over the spire of St. Paul's; nor does
it exhibit the slightest deviation from one
invariable poetic mind and temperament.
Shakespeare's fancy takes a free range here,
and revels in beauty and joy. The Dream
was first published in 1600; the earliest

allusion made to it is that of Francis Meres, in *Palladis Tamia*, in 1598; and probably it was written as early as 1594, when Shakespeare was thirty years old. A significant reference to the subject of it occurs in the second scene of the second act of the *Comedy of Errors* (1589–1591), which has been thought to indicate that the poet had already considered and perhaps conceived it: he was working with wise and incessant industry at that time, and the amazing fertility of his creative genius was beginning to reveal itself. The Dream is absolutely of his own invention. The names of the characters, together with a few incidents, he derived from Plutarch, Ovid, and Chaucer — authors with whom he shows himself to have been acquainted. The story of Pyramus and Thisbe occurs in Ovid, and a translation of that Latin poet, made by Arthur Golding, was current in Shakespeare's day. It is thought that the *Knight's Tale* and *Tysbe of Babylone*, by Chaucer, may have been the means of suggesting this play to Shakespeare, but his story and his characters are his own. And although, as Dr. Johnson observes, fairies were in his time fashionable, and Spenser's *Faerie Queene* had made them great, Shakespeare

was the first to interblend them with the
proceedings of mortals in a drama. The
text of the piece is considered to be exceptionally free from error or any sort of
defect. Two editions of the Dream, quarto,
appeared in 1600 — one published by Thomas
Fisher, bookseller; the other by James
Roberts, printer. The Fisher publication
had been entered at Stationers' Hall, October 8, that year, and probably it was sanc-
tioned by the author. The two editions do
not materially differ, and the modern
Shakespearean editors have made a judicious
use of both in their choice of the text.
The play was not again printed until 1623,
when it appeared in the first folio. It is
not known which was first of the Fisher
and the Roberts quartos, or which was
authorised. Each of those quartos consists
of 32 leaves. Neither of them distinguishes
the acts or scenes. In the first folio
(1623) the Dream occupies 18 pages, from
p. 145 to p. 162 inclusive, in the section
devoted to comedies — the acts, but not the
scenes, being distinguished. The editors
of that folio, Heminge and Condell, followed the text of the Roberts quarto. The
memory of one of the actors who appeared
in the Dream in its earliest days is curi-

ously preserved in a stage-direction, printed
in the first folio, in Act v., sc. i.: "Tawyer
with a trumpet." The piece appears in
the later folios, — 1632, 1663–64, and 1685.
A Midsummer Night's Dream was popular
in Shakespeare's time. Mention of it, as
impliedly a play in general knowledge and
acceptance, was made by Taylor, the water
poet, in 1622.

A piece called *The Fairy Queen*, being
Shakespeare's comedy, with music by Purcell,[1] was published in London in 1692. It
had been acted there, at the Haymarket —
the presentation being made with fine
scenery and elaborate mechanism. There
is another old piece, called *The Merry-Con-
ceited Humours of Bottom the Weaver*.
This was made out of an episode in the
Dream, and it is included in the collection
of farces attributed to Robert Cox, a comedian of the time of Charles I., published in
1672. A comic masque, by Richard Lever-
idge, similarly derived, entitled *Pyramus
and Thisbe*, was performed at Lincoln's
Inn Fields theatre, and was published in
1716. Two other musical farces, with this
same title and origin, are recorded — one

---

[1] Henry Purcell, 1658–1695, and Thomas Purcell,
——–1682, were both musical composers.

by Mr. Lampe, acted at Covent Garden,
and published in 1745 ; the other by W. C.
Oulton, acted at Birmingham, and published in 1798. Garrick made an acting
copy of *A Midsummer Night's Dream* —
adding to the text as well as curtailing it,
and introducing songs — and this was played
at Drury Lane, where it failed, and was
published in 1763. Colman reduced Garrick's piece to two acts, and called it *A
Fairy Tale*, and in this form it was tried at
Drury Lane, and published in 1764 and
1777. Colman, however, wrote : " I was
little more than a godfather on the occasion,
and the alterations should have been sub-
scribed Anon." The best production of
this comedy ever accomplished on the English stage was that effected by Charles
Kean, at the Princess's theatre, London, —
managed by him from August 1850 till
August 29, 1859.

The first performance of *A Midsummer
Night's Dream* given in America occurred
at the old Park theatre, for the benefit of Mrs. Hilson, on November 9, 1826.
Ireland, in his valuable records, has preserved a part of the cast, rescued from a
mutilated copy of the playbill of that night :
Theseus, Mr. Lee ; Bottom, Mr. Hilson ;

Snout, Mr. Placide; Oberon, Peter Richings; Puck, Mrs. Hilson; Titania, Mrs.
Sharpe; Hippolita, Mrs. Stickney; Hermia,
Mrs. Hackett. On August 30, 1841 the
comedy was again revived at that theatre,
with a cast that included Mr. Fredericks
as Theseus, W. H. Williams as Bottom,
Mrs. Knight as Puck, Charlotte Cushman
as Oberon, Mary Taylor as Titania, Susan
Cushman as Helena, Mrs. Groves as Hippolita, Miss Buloid (afterward Mrs. Abbott)
as Hermia, and William Wheatley as Lysander. The next revivals came on February 3 and 6, 1854, at Burton's theatre and
at the Broadway theatre, rival houses, with
these casts:

	At Broadway.	At Burton's.
Theseus....	F. B. Conway.......	Charles Fisher.
Lysander...	Lannergan..........	George Jordan.
Demetrius..	Grosvenor..........	W. H. Norton.
Egeus......	Matthews...........	Moore.
Bottom.....	William Davidge....	W. E. Burton.
Quince.....	Howard..........	T. Johnston.
Flute......	Whiting............	G. Barrett.
Snug.......	Fisk................	Russell.
Snout......	Henry..............	G. Andrews.
Puck.......	Viola Crocker......	Parsloe.
Oberon.....	Mme. Ponisi........	Miss E. Raymond.
Titania....	Mrs. Abbott........	Mrs. Burton.
Hippolita...	Mrs. Warren........	Mrs. J. Cooke.
Hermia.....	Mrs. Nagle.........	Mrs. Hough.
Helena.....	A. Gougenheim......	Mrs. Buckland.

Great stress, in both cases, was laid upon Mendelssohn's music. At each house it ran for a month. It was not revived in New York again until April 18, 1859, when Laura Keene brought it forward at her theatre, and kept it on till May 28, with C. W. Couldock as Theseus, William Rufus Blake as Bottom, Miss Macarthy as Oberon, Miss Stevens as Helena, Ada Clifton as Hermia, and herself as Puck. It was a failure. Even Blake failed as Bottom, — an acute critic of that period, Edward G. P. Wilkins, describing the performance as "not funny, not even grotesque, but vulgar and unpleasant." Charles Peters was good as Thisbe. The stage version used was made by Richard Grant White. That same theatre subsequently became the Olympic (not Mitchell's, but the second of that name), and there, on October 28, 1867, under the management of James E. Hayes and the direction of Joseph Jefferson, who had brought from London a Grecian panorama by Telbin, *A Midsummer Night's Dream* was again offered, with a cast that included G. L. Fox as Bottom, W. Davidge as Quince, Owen Marlowe as Flute, Cornelia Jefferson as Titania, and Clara Fisher as Peasblossom. Telbin's panorama displayed the country supposed to lie between Athens and the forest wherein the Fairy Queen and the lovers are enchanted and bewitched and the sapient Bottom is "translated." Fox undertook Bottom, for the first time, and he was drolly consequential and stolidly conceited in it. Landseer's famous picture of Titania and the ass-headed Bottom was copied in one of the scenes. Mr. Hayes provided a shining tableau at the close. Mendelssohn's music was played and sung, with excellent skill and effect — the chief vocalist being Clara Fisher. Owen Marlowe, as Thisbe, gave a burlesque of the manner of Rachel. The comedy, as then given, ran for one hundred nights — from October 28, 1867 till February 1, 1868. The stage version used was that of Charles Kean.

The next production of *A Midsummer Night's Dream* was effected by Augustin Daly, at the Grand Opera House, on August 19, 1873. The scenery then employed was of extraordinary beauty — delicate in colour, sensuous in feeling, sprightly in fancy. Fox again played Bottom. The attentive observer of the stage version made by Augustin Daly, — and conspicu-

ously used by him when he revived the
piece at his theatre on January 31, 1888, —
would observe that much new and effective
stage business was introduced. The disposition of the groups at the start was fresh, and
so was the treatment of the quarrel between
Oberon and Titania, with the disappearance of the Indian child. The moonlight
effects, in the transition from act second
to act third, and the gradual assembly
of goblins and fairies in shadowy mists
through which the fire-flies glimmered, at the
close of act third, were novel and beautiful.
Cuts and transpositions were made at the
end of the fourth act, in order to close
it with the voyage of the barge of Theseus,
through a summer landscape, on the silver
stream that rippled down to Athens. The
third act was judiciously compressed, so
that the spectator might not see too much
of the perplexed and wrangling lovers.
But little of the original text was omitted.
The music for the choruses was selected
from various English composers — that of
Mendelssohn being prescribed only for the
orchestra.

The accepted doctrine of traditional
criticism — a doctrine made seemingly potent by reiteration — that A *Midsummer*

Night's Dream is not for the stage, need not necessarily be considered final. Hazlitt was the first to insist on that idea. "Poetry and the stage," said that famous writer, "do not agree well together. The attempt to reconcile them, in this instance, fails not only of effect, but of decorum. The ideal can have no place upon the stage, which is a picture without perspective. The imagination cannot sufficiently qualify the actual impression of the senses." But this is only saying that there are difficulties. The remark applies to all the higher forms of dramatic literature ; and, logically, if that doctrine were observed in practice, none of the great plays would be attempted. *A Midsummer Night's Dream*, with all its ideal spirit, is dramatic ; it ought not to be lost to the stage ; and to some extent, certainly, the difficulties can be surmounted. In the spirit of a dream the play was written, and in the spirit of a dream it can be acted.

The student of *A Midsummer Night's Dream*, as often as he thinks upon that lofty and lovely expression of a luxuriant and happy poetic fancy, must necessarily find himself impressed with its exquisite purity of spirit, its affluence of invention, its extraordinary wealth of contrasted characters, its absolute symmetry of form, and its great beauty of poetic diction. The essential cleanliness and sweetness of Shakespeare's mind, unaffected by the gross animalism of his time, appear conspicuously in that play. No single trait of the piece impresses the reader more agreeably than its frank display of the spontaneous, natural, and entirely delightful exultation of Theseus and Hippolita in their approaching nuptials. They are grand creatures, and they rejoice in each other and in their perfectly accordant love. Nowhere in Shakespeare is there a more imperial man than Theseus; nor, despite her feminine impatience of dulness, a woman more royal and more essentially woman-like than Hippolita. It is thought that the immediate impulse of that comedy, in Shakespeare's mind, was the marriage of his friend and benefactor the Earl of Southampton with Elizabeth Vernon — which, while it did not in fact occur till 1598, was probably agreed upon, and had received Queen Elizabeth's sanction, as early as 1594–95. In old English literature it is seen that such a theme often proved suggestive of ribaldry; but Shakespeare could preserve the sanc-

tity even while he revelled in the passionate ardour of love; and *A Midsummer
Night's Dream*, while it possesses the rosy
glow, the physical thrill, and the melting
tenderness of such pieces as Herrick's
Nuptiall Song, is likewise fraught with the
moral elevation and unaffected chastity of
such pieces as Milton's *Comus*. Human
nature is shown in it as feeling no shame
in its elemental passions, and as having no
reason to feel ashamed of them. The atmosphere is free and bracing; the tone
honest; the note true. Then, likewise,
the fertility and felicity of the poet's invention — intertwining the loves of earthly
sovereigns and of their subjects with the
dissensions of fairy monarchs, the pranks
of mischievous elves, the protective care of
attendant sprites, and the comic but kind-
hearted and well-meant fealty of boorish
peasants — arouse lively interest and keep
it steadily alert. In no other one of his
works has Shakespeare more brilliantly
shown that complete dominance of theme
which is manifested in the perfect preser-
vation of proportion. The strands of action
are braided with astonishing grace. The
fourfold story is never allowed to lapse
into dulness or obscurity. There is caprice,

M

but no distortion. The supernatural ma-
chinery is never wrested toward the production of startling or monstrous effects,
but it deftly impels each mortal personage
in the natural line of human development.
The dream-spirit is maintained throughout, and perhaps it is for that reason —
that the poet was living, thinking, writing
in the free, untrammelled world of his
spacious and airy imagination and not in
any definite sphere of this earth — that *A
Midsummer Night's Dream* is radically
superior to the other comedies written
by him at about the same period, *The
Two Gentlemen of Verona, The Comedy of
Errors, Love's Labour's Lost,* and *The
Taming of the Shrew.* His genius over-
flows in this piece, and the rich excess
of it is seen in passages of exquisite
poetry — such as the beautiful speeches of
Titania and Oberon, in the second act —
over against which is set that triumph of
humour, that immortal Interlude of *Pyramus and Thisbe,* which is the father of all
the burlesques in our language, and which,
for freshness, pungency of apposite satire,
and general applicability to the foible of
self-love in human nature and to igno-
rance and folly in human affairs, might

have been written yesterday. The only
faults in this play are a slight tinge of
monotony in the third act, concerning the
lovers in the wood, and an excess of
rhymed passages in the text throughout.
Shakespeare had not yet cast aside that
custom of rhyme which was in vogue when
he came first upon the scene. But those
defects are trifles. The beauties overwhelm
them. It would take many pages to enu-
merate and fitly to descant on the felicities
of literature that we owe to this comedy —
gems such as the famous passage on "the
course of true love"; the regal picture of
Queen Elizabeth as "a fair vestal throned
by the west"; the fine description of the
stormy summer (that of 1594 in England,
according to Stow's *Chronicle* and Dr.
Simon Forman's *Diary*); the vision of
Titania asleep upon the bank of wild
thyme, oxlips, and violets; the eloquent
contrasts of lover, madman, and poet, each
subdued and impelled by that "strong
imagination" which "bodies forth the
forms of things unknown"; and the wonderfully spirited lines on the hounds of
Sparta, — "with ears that swept away the
morning dew." In character likewise, and
in those salutary lessons that the truthful

portraiture of character invariably teaches,
this piece is exceptionally strong. Helena,
noble and loving, yet a little perverted
from dignity by her sexual infatuation;
Hermia, shrewish and violent, despite her
feminine sweetness, and possibly because
of her impetuous and clinging ardour;
Demetrius and Lysander, each selfish and
fierce in his love, but manly, straightfor-
ward fellows, abounding more in youth
and desire than in brains; Bottom, the
quintessence of bland, unconscious egotism
and self-conceit; and Theseus, the princely
gentleman and typical ruler — these make
up one of the most interesting and significant groups that can be found in fiction.
The self-centred nature, the broad-minded
view, the magnanimous spirit, the calm
adequacy, the fine and high manner of
Theseus, make that character alone the
inspiration of the comedy and a most
potent lesson upon the conduct of life.
Through certain of his people — such as
Ulysses in *Troilus and Cressida*, the Duke
in *Measure for Measure*, and Prospero in
The Tempest — the voice of Shakespeare
himself, speaking personally, is clearly
heard; and it is heard also in Theseus.
"The best in this kind are but shadows,"

says that wise observer of life, when he comes to speak of the actors who copy it, "and the worst are no worse, if imagination amend them." There is no higher strain of princelike courtesy and considerate grace, even in the perfect breeding of Hamlet, than is visible in the preference of Theseus for the play of the hard-handed men of Athens : —

> "Never anything can be amiss
> When simpleness and duty tender it. . . .
> And what poor duty cannot do
> Noble respect takes it in might, not merit."

With reference to the question of suitable method in the acting of *A Midsummer Night's Dream* it may be observed that too much stress can scarcely be laid upon the fact that this comedy was conceived and written absolutely in the spirit of a dream. It ought not, therefore, to be treated as a rational manifestation of orderly design. It possesses, indeed, a coherent and symmetrical plot and a definite purpose; but, while it moves toward a final result of absolute order, it presupposes intermediary progress through a realm of motley shapes and fantastic vision. Its persons are creatures of the fancy, and all effort to make them

solidly actual, to set them firmly upon the
earth, and to accept them as realities of
common life, is labour ill-bestowed. To
body forth the form of things is, in this
case, manifestly, a difficult task : and yet
the true course is obvious. Actors who
yield themselves to the spirit of whim, and
drift along with it, using a delicate method
and avoiding insistence upon prosy realism,
will succeed with this piece — provided,
also, that their audience can be fanciful,
and can accept the performance, not as a
comedy of ordinary life but as a vision seen
in a dream. The play is full of intimations
that this was Shakespeare's mood. Even
Bottom, the consummate flower of unconscious humour, is at his height of significance in his moment of supreme illusion :
" I have had a dream, — past the wit of
man to say what dream it was : — Man is
but an ass if he go about to expound this
dream. Methought I was — there is no
man can tell what. Methought I was, and
methought I had — But man is but a
patched fool if he will offer to say what methought I had. The eye of man hath not
heard, the ear of man hath not seen, man's
hand is not able to taste, his tongue to con-
ceive, nor his heart to report, what my

dream was." The whole philosophy of the
subject, comically stated, is there. A serious
statement of it is in the words of the poet
Campbell : —

" Well may sleep present us fictions,
    Since our waking moments teem
    With such fanciful convictions
    As make life itself a dream."

Various actors in the past — although *A
Midsummer Night's Dream* has not had
great currency upon the stage, at any period,
whether in England or America — have laid
a marked stress upon the character of
Bottom. Samuel Phelps, upon the London
stage, was esteemed excellent in it. He
acted the part in his production of the
Dream, at Sadler's Wells, and he again
acted it in 1870 at the Queen's theatre, in
Long Acre — now demolished. On the
American stage William E. Burton was accounted wonderfully good in it. " As Burton renders the character," says Richard
Grant White, " its traits are brought out
with a delicate and masterly hand ; its
humour is exquisite." And William L.
Keese, in his careful biography of Burton,
makes equally cordial reference to that
achievement of the great comedian : " How

striking it was in sustained individuality, and how finely exemplified was the potential vanity of Bottom! What pleased us greatly was the vein of engaging raillery which ran through the delivery of his speeches to the fairies." Burton produced the Dream at his theatre, in 1854, with such wealth of fine scenery as in those days was accounted prodigious. The most notable impersonation of Bottom that has been given since Burton's time was, probably, that of George L. Fox. Self-conceit, as the essence of the character, was thoroughly well understood and expressed by him. He wore the ass's head, but he did not know that he was wearing it ; and when, afterward, the vague sense of it came upon him for an instant, he put it by as something inconceivable and intolerable. His " Not a word of me ! " — spoken to the cther hard-handed men of Athens, after his return to them out of the enchanted " palace wood " — was his finest single point. Certainly it expressed to the utmost the colossal self-love and swelling pomposity of this miracle of bland and opaque sapience. The essential need of acting, in a portrayal of this play, is whimsicality — but it must be whimsicality exalted by poetry.

It is remarked by Hazlitt that "the stage is an epitome, a bettered likeness of the world, with the dull part left out"; and the fine thinker adds, with subtle insight and quaint wisdom, that "indeed, with this omission, it is nearly big enough to hold all the rest." There is a profound and significant truth in that observation. Actual life, in most of its aspects, is dull and tedious. Almost all persons are commonplace — except at moments. Almost all scenes are insipid — except at moments. Nature will not show herself to you at all times. The glory of sunrise is revealed only once in a day, and even then you will not see it unless you are in the right mood. The uncommon element in human creatures must be awakened before they can really discern anything. Most persons who have reached middle age know absolutely nothing that is worth knowing except what they saw during the one brief, sweet, youthful hour when they were in love. It is the uncommon element that endows man with perception, and it is the uncommon element that makes humanity interesting. Common life is barren; and sometimes it is worse than barren — because the contemplation of it is extremely apt to engender a bitter contempt for humanity, as altogether vacuous, frivolous, and trivial. The world of art has no room for the commonplace. No properly organised mind will ever be contented with a photograph if it can get anything better. We do not wish to know what people are, in their ordinary state. We know, only too well, that human nature, in its average condition, is full of selfishness, envy, malice, and greed. There is no circle into which any man enters, anywhere, in which he does not invariably hear people, sooner or later, speaking ill of other people behind their backs. Detraction is universal and it is perennial. We do not wish in art, or in anything else, to hear the small talk, the cackle, the babble of everyday life. Humanity should be contemplated in its idealised aspects. Shakespeare has endured, and he will endure forever (not, perhaps, upon the stage, from which an effort is already in formidable progress to exclude him, as being archaic and not contemporaneous), because, while absolutely true to truth in his reflections of human nature, he idealised and transfigured it.

XIII.

WILL O' THE WISP: LOVE'S LABOUR'S LOST.

THE subject of this comedy is self-culture — a subject that commends itself to the attention of young men, and one that has frequently been treated by young authors. Shakespeare obviously was a young author when he wrote *Love's Labour's Lost;* yet in this case, while the subject has been viewed with youthful enthusiasm, it has also been viewed with the intuition of genius. The idea of natural development that lies imbedded in the structure of this work is absolutely sound and true. Mental cultivation is a noble pursuit (so Shakespeare seems now to declare), but the nature of man is not exclusively intellectual; it is also physical and spiritual; it comprises passions and affections. Man was not intended to live a monastic life. Love is in this world, as well as Thought, and the true conduct of existence will not be ascetic, but vital, free, simple, cheerful, and happy.

The King of Navarre and his three chosen lords, Biron, Longaville, and Dumain — who typify at first a favourite theory of youth, the theory of exclusive devotion to the ideal — may seclude themselves as carefully as they please; but they will presently find that rebellion flows in their blood, and as soon as woman comes upon the scene of their retreat — as inevitably she will come — their cool, stately, scholastic, but tepid, barren, and insincere reserve will be ludicrously broken and defeated. This evidently is all that the play was intended to mean, and this meaning it conveys, intermingled with satire on certain social foibles of Shakespeare's early day, in a forcible, direct manner, and in a spirit of pungent truth which neither youthful effusiveness nor immaturity of style is potent to invalidate. As far as he could go without much experience Shakespeare went in *Love's Labour's Lost*. After he had gained his experience he went much further; but it was still in the same line — as the student sees in *Much Ado About Nothing*.

The story of this comedy is pretty and pleasing, but the piece does not contain many incidents, and the element of action in it is less prominent than are the elements

of poetry and humour. Ferdinand, King of
Navarre, and his three lords dedicate themselves, for three years, to study. They are
to dwell alone. They are to be frugal and
vigilant.   They are to refrain from the
society of ladies. They are to be temperate,
placid, chaste, pure, and cold. In a word,
they are to be dedicated to Mind. The
King of Navarre, however, is obliged to
receive a visit from the Princess of France,
who comes to him as an ambassador from
her royal father, on a political mission, and
who is accompanied by three of her ladies,
Rosaline, Maria, and Katharine. These
are handsome young women, and as soon
as they invade Navarre's serene retreat the
four consecrated young men incontinently
fall in love with them, and each endeavours
to press his suit in secret. All are thus for-
sworn, and much merriment is extracted
from the expedient of making each of them
betray his secret to the others, until they
all stand in comic discomfiture together.
At the last the condemnation of their error
in making a foolish compact is frankly
spoken, and in words of signal eloquence
and beauty, by the wisest and merriest of
them, Biron (in the old copies of the play
this name is given as Berowne), who from the

first has only humoured Navarre's caprice
for monasticism but has never believed in
its wisdom.   Those lovers are much teased
and tantalised by the sparkling French
girls, when their droll predicament is disclosed; but in each case, happily, the love
of the youths is reciprocated, and so a comfortable pairing time is seen to be imminent;
when suddenly comes news that the royal
father of the Princess has died.   There can
be no nuptials now, for a year.   Love's
labour is lost.   The enamoured King of
Navarre must prove his fidelity by patience.
The frolicsome Biron must tend the sick
for a twelvemonth and show himself something better than a farceur, in order to be
worthy of his Rosaline.   In the under plot,
which is suffused with eccentric humour, the
fantastical Spaniard, Armado, held in
amorous captivity by the country wench,
Jaquenetta, affords a more broadly comical
illustration of the central truth which ani-
mates this play.   No man can escape from
the doom of love.

> "Nature her custom holds,
>   Let shame say what it will."

Love's Labour's Lost is pure invention.
"The story of it," says Steevens, "has

most of the features of an ancient romance."
"It would be more correct to say," observes Charles Knight, "that it has most
of the features which would be derived from
an acquaintance with the ancient romances."
There was no Ferdinand, King of Navarre,
and there is no record that any question
was ever raised between France and Navarre with reference to possessions in
Aquitain — the settlement of which is the
ostensible object of the Princess's visit to
Ferdinand's court. The scene is laid in
Navarre. The time is Shakespeare's time ;
and the piece has, accordingly, to be attired
for the stage in the styles of raiment peculiar to the period of Henry IV. of France
(1553–1610), and Philip II. of Spain (1527–
1598). The comedy drift in Shakespeare's
mind, from the outset till the last, is distinctly indicated in this piece. Biron and
Rosaline are the precursors of Benedick
and Beatrice. Armado is the germ of Mal-
volio. Jaquenetta is a faint prelude both
to Maria and Audrey. Dull gives a hint of
the future Dogberry. In Holofernes, the
schoolmaster — who foreshadows Sir Hugh
Evans — some commentators have discovered a satirical portraiture of John Florio,
one of Shakespeare's contemporaries, who

taught Italian in London, and made a dictionary of that language called *A World of Words;* but no conclusive evidence has been adduced to sustain that notion. Holofernes is Shakespeare's satire on ridiculous pedantry, just as Armado is his satire on ridiculous affectation, pomposity, and conceit. Against those foolish things he places, in beautiful contrast, his delicious rural melodies — " When daisies pied and violets blue," and " When icicles hang by the wall," — and the listener feels indeed that " the words of Mercury are harsh after the songs of Apollo."

Fifteen of Shakespeare's thirty-seven plays were published in his lifetime, the comedy of *Love's Labour's Lost* being one of them. The title of the first edition, quarto, is : " A pleasant conceited comedie called Loues Labors Lost. As it was presented before her Highnes this last Christmas. Newly corrected and augmented by W. Shakespeare. Imprinted at London by W. W. for Cutbert Burly, 1598." The Highness indicated is Queen Elizabeth (1558–1603), and the Christmas that of 1597. In the first folio of Shakespeare (1623) the text of this piece is the text of the quarto, allowing for merely accidental discrepancies. The errors of the quarto, which are numerous, reappear in the folio. Heminge and Condell, when they say "we have scarce received from him" [Shakespeare] "a blot in his papers," are not to be taken too literally. They possibly possessed some of Shakespeare's manuscripts and they may have used them as "copy" for the printer; but their folio seems to show that they must have used as "copy" some of the prompt-books of Shakespeare's plays, obtained from the theatre — such books as may have survived the destructive fire at the Globe in 1613 — together with several of the early quartos. No one knows what has become of Shakespeare's "papers" — or, indeed, of the papers of some other authors of Shakespeare's time. The early quartos exist; but no prompt-book has been found, nor any piece of manuscript. It is not unlikely that much if not the whole mass of the printer's "copy" that was used in setting up the folio of 1623 was heedlessly dispersed and destroyed in the printing-office, after the completion of that work. In those days no such care was taken, as to matters of this sort, as is habitually taken now. The reprint in the folio of *Love's Labour's Lost* must cer-

tainly have been made from the quarto, for
both contain, in Act v. sc. 2, the lines,
827 to 832, beginning "You must be purgéd
too, your sins are rank" — that are, by
Coleridge and others, judiciously deemed a
superfluous fragment from the first draft of
the piece; and also the lines in Biron's
speech, in Act iv. sc. 3, that are immediately repeated in an altered form. (Lines
296–317; paraphrased in lines 318–354.)[1]
The title of the piece is questioned. Some
editors of the poet call it *Love's Labour
Lost;* others prefer *Love's Labours Lost;*
and still others declare for *Love's Labour
is Lost.* In the title of the quarto no apos-
trophe is used. In the folio of 1623 the
play is called *Loues Labour's Lost.* In
every form the idea remains the same. It
has been alleged that the fashion of speech
called Euphuism, which was prevalent in

---

[1] Capell sagaciously saw that in this speech, from
"For where would you" to "From whence doth
spring," and from "For where is any" to "And in
that vow," are passages which the poet had cancelled
in the "corrected and augmented" play. The same
occurs in *Richard III.*, v. 3, and, on a much
smaller scale, however, in *Romeo and Juliet*, iii.
3, iv. 1. — KEIGHTLEY. — This is another trouble
for the makers of "cyphers" — as Prof. Rolfe has
pungently suggested; for the validity of a "cypher"
is vitally dependent on a perfectly accurate text.

polite society in the reign of Gloriana (*Eupheus, the Anatomy of Wit*, by John Lilly, was published in 1580 and *Eupheus and his England* in 1581), was the particular object of Shakespeare's satire — as indicated in the character of Don Adriano de Armado ; but it seems more likely that he was writing out of a natural, humorous scorn of artificiality and pomposity, and with the recollection of his early reading still fresh in mind. Coleridge — perhaps the wisest thinker that ever wrote on Shakespeare — says : " It is not unimportant to notice how strong a presumption the diction and allusions of this play afford that, though Shakespeare's acquirements in the dead languages might not be such as we suppose in a learned education, his habits had nevertheless been scholastic and those of a student. For a young author's first work almost always bespeaks his recent pursuits ; and his first observations of life are either drawn from the immediate employments of his youth and from the characters and images most deeply impressed on his mind in the situation in which those employments have placed him, or else they are fixed on such objects and occurrences in the world as are easily connected with, and seem to

bear upon, his studies and the hitherto
exclusive subjects of his meditations."

In all examination into the writings of
Shakespeare the student naturally likes to
approach as nearly as possible to the personality of that wonderful poet. *Love's
Labour's Lost* suggests him as he was at
the beginning of his career. There is no
immaturity, indeed, in the mental substance of the piece, in its drift of thought,
in its conviction that no artificial scheme of
frigid self-denial can withstand the pur-
poses of nature. "Young blood will but
obey an old decree." The immaturity is
mostly in the style, and it is shown in the
frequency of rhymed passages, in the capricious mutations of the verse, and in the
florid metaphor and the tumultuous sentiment. When completely formed the style
of Shakespeare, while possessing the flexibility of the finest-tempered steel, possesses
also its uniform solidity and strength.
Throughout much of the language of this
comedy there is a lack of the power of self-
knowledge and self-restraint. Parts of the
text are, indeed, full of sinew and tremu-
lous with intellectual vitality. No doubt
the author retouched it when he "newly
corrected and augmented" the piece for the

press in 1598 — when he was thirty-four
years old and in full vigour. Biron's fine
speech in Act. iv., "Have at ye then,
affection's men at arms," was probably
rewritten at that time. Yet parts of the
text are diffuse and strained, and in the
contemplation of these the best Shakespeare scholars agree that the first draft of
the comedy must have been written when
the author was a youth. This view is con-
firmed by the fact that it is at once sentimental and satirical; that it deals with that
extremely ambitious theme, the conduct of
life; that it assails conventional affecta-
tions; and that it is reformatory in spirit
and would set matters right. That kind of
zeal belongs to the springtime of the human
mind, and it seldom endures. *Love's Labour's Lost* was probably written as early
as 1590, and it may well have preceded
The Two Gentlemen of Verona, which is
commonly set down as Shakespeare's first
comedy. He had begun by altering and
improving older plays — the kind of work
that he accomplished in that vein being
exemplified by *Pericles*, *Titus Andronicus*,
and a portion of *Henry VI*. But he soon
entered on a pathway exclusively his own.
He never hesitated to make use of hints

derived from earlier or from contemporaneous works, either histories or fictions; but whatever he touched was transfigured and became new and original in his treatment of it and in his unique and potent style. *Love's Labour's Lost* is entirely original. "It is apparently wholly our poet's own invention," says the judicious Keightley, "as no novel, play, or anything else, at all resembling it, has been discovered." Another and an equally significant fact is that it was the first of his published plays that bore on the title-page the illustrious name of Shakespeare.

The eccentric persons who are anxious to convince themselves that the works of Shakespeare were written by somebody else might perhaps be restrained if they would ponder a little on these facts. The earliest existing mention of Shakespeare by name is a mention made in the accounts of the Treasurer of the Chamber, showing that he was a member of the Lord Chamberlain's company of actors, and that he twice appeared with Richard Burbage before Queen Elizabeth, at Christmas 1594 — in his thirty-first year. This fact shows his rank as an actor. The later mention of him, made by Meres in *Palladis Tamia*, 1598, shows that

he had also been fertile and successful
as a dramatic author. "As Plautus and
Seneca are accounted the best for Comedy
and Tragedy among the Latines," says
Meres, " so Shakespeare among the English
is the most excellent in both kinds for the
stage : for Comedy, witness his Gentlemen
of Verona, his Errors, his Love labors lost,
his Love labours wonne, his Midsummer's
night dreame, and his Merchant of Venice ;
for Tragedy, his Richard the 2, Richard the
3, Henry the 4, King John, Titus Andronicus, and his Romeo and Juliet." The plays
thus named must have been produced upon
the stage prior to 1598. They were accepted,
not as the work of an unknown, mysterious
author, but as the work of William Shakespeare, then and there present and visible
and in continual social and professional in-
tercourse with the actors and writers of the
time, and with numbers of its great people.
This period is six years later than Greene's
malevolent allusion to the "upstart crow,"
" in his own conceit the onely Shakescene
in a country," and to Henry Chettle's se-
quent apology for having published Greene's
rancorous and offensive though puerile im-
pertinence. " I am as sorry," says the pub-
lisher of the *Groatsworth of Wit*, " as if the

original fault had beene my fault, because
myselfe have seene his demeanour no lesse
civill than he exelent in the qualitie he pro-
fesses ; besides divers of worship have re-
ported his uprightnes of dealing, which
argues his honesty, and his facetious grace
in writting, that aprooves his art." Shakespeare was an accomplished and esteemed
gentleman, an excellent actor, and a felicitous writer (facetious in those days meaning felicitous). Meres, mindful of rhetorical
balance and careless of thoroughness, naming six tragedies and six comedies, obviously
intended to refer to an even number of each
kind of play : but Shakespeare, prior to the
date of *Palladis Tamia*, had not only written
the works that have been mentioned, but
had written the *Taming of the Shrew* and
the first part of *Henry the Fourth*. He was
eminent among the authors of his time —
well rewarded, prosperous, honoured, and,
as may be surmised by the reader of Ben
Jonson's *Conversations* with Drummond,
closely observed in all his walks and ways ;
a man of publicity and distinction — and
the comedy of *Love's Labour's Lost* had
helped to make him so.

In what degree the piece had popularity
in its immediate day no one now can tell.

Its bearing as a local and contemporary
satire ought to have made it successful.
The public has always disliked satire and
satirists, and at the same time has always,
for a while, followed them and favoured
them. Its admirably humorous scene of
the discovery that all the dedicated celi-
bates are in love, and its subsequent
sprightly colloquies of raillery in which
those wooers are chaffed by the merry
maidens of France, would have pleased
any audience at any time; and doubtless
those merits were appreciated by the gal-
lants of Gloriana's court. It seems, however, soon to have vanished from the stage.
In his chapter entitled "Plays Printed But
Not Acted, Between 1660 and 1830" Genest makes the following note on a play
called *The Students*, printed in 1762:
"STUDENTS, 1762. This is professedly
Love's Labour Lost, adapted to the stage,
but it does not seem to have been ever
acted. The maker of the alteration, as is
usual in these cases, has left out too much
of Shakespeare and put in too much of his
own stuff. Biron is foolishly made to put
on Costard's coat; in this disguise he
speaks part of what belongs to Costard,
and is mistaken for him by several of the

characters. The curate and schoolmaster are omitted, but one of the pedantic speeches belonging to the latter is absurdly given to a player. One thing is very happily altered: Armado's letter to the King is omitted as a letter, and the contents of it are thrown into Armado's part. The Cuckow Song is transferred from the end of the play to the second act, in which it is sung by Moth. It is now usually sung in *As You Like It*. Steevens, in a note on the third act of the original play, observes that in many of the old comedies the songs are frequently omitted. On this occasion the stage direction is generally, Here they sing, or cantant. Probably the performer was left to the choice of his own ditty. Sometimes yet more was left to the discretion of the ancient comedians. Thus, in Greene's *Tu Quoque*, 'Here they two talk and rail what they list.' Steevens gives other similar instances."

When Shakespeare first arrived in London (1585–86) only two notable public playhouses were open in that city. Those were the Theatre, managed by his townsman James Burbage, in Finsbury Field, and the Curtain, in Shoreditch. Both are mentioned by Stow (1525–1605), and both certainly existed as early as 1583. The Blackfriars (erected in 1570) was a private theatre ; but it seems to have become a public one in 1597. The Globe was opened in 1599, and it was burnt down on June 29, 1613. The Rose was opened by Henslowe, in February 1591, "on the Bancksyde" — that is, at Southwark. Most of Shakespeare's plays were originally produced at one or another of those theatres. It is probable that the first performance of *Love's Labour's Lost* occurred at the Rose ; though it may have been at the Curtain.

In all the long annals of the British and American drama there is but scant record of any considerable revivals of this comedy. It was performed in London, at Covent Garden, in September 1839, when Eliza Vestris acted Rosaline and the beautiful Louisa Nisbett acted the Princess of France. That earnest, intrepid, thorough actor, Samuel Phelps, revived it at Sadler's Wells, London, in 1857. It was included by Charles Edward Flower in his tasteful and useful edition of Shakespeare's plays prepared for representation in the Memorial theatre at Stratford-upon-Avon. It was presented at the Arch Street theatre, Philadelphia, in 1858, but that revival seems to have been one of transient value. The first practically auspicious reproduction of it that the student comes upon, in modern theatrical chronicles, is that made by Augustin Daly, when his theatre (then called the Fifth Avenue) was in Twenty-eighth street, New York, on February 21, 1874. It had not until then been acted on the New York stage, and after that it slumbered for seventeen years, till revived by the same manager, on March 28, 1891, with Ada Rehan as the Princess.

The careful student of Shakespeare's methods will not fail to observe that in *Love's Labour's Lost* the poet has taken the same course that he pursues in *A Midsummer Night's Dream*, and also that in this early comedy he presages the form of all his later ones. In both the *Dream* and the *Labour* the persons who are distinctively humorous conjoin at last in giving an entertainment of a dramatic character, in the presence of royalty and nobility. In the former we have Pyramus and Thisbe; in the latter the Pageant of the Nine Worthies. By this device the poet effects the most ample disclosure of his eccentric people — showing more fully what they are by making them show what they think themselves to be. The humorous part of *Love's Labour's Lost* is the richest part of it. The vein of quaint, quizzical, fantastic drollery in Shakespeare's nature showed itself early to be deep and rich, and his wonderful command of humorous phraseology was also brilliantly shown in that piece. The intensely English character of the man, together with his complete carelessness of accurate and formal scholarship — a qualification which he did not possess, and which he would not have regarded even if he had possessed it — are also visible in the humorous part of *Love's Labour's Lost*. Every point, howsoever slight, has to be considered in the study of an author about whose personality our chief information has necessarily to be derived from the analysis of his mind. The fact that into *Love's Labour's Lost*, although the scene is laid in Navarre, the poet introduced such names and persons as Costard, Dull, and Moth is, therefore, not devoid of significance. In arranging *Love's Labour's Lost* for the stage the editor condensed it, and blended the third act, which in the original is very short, with the essential portions of the fourth. Allusion to the death of the French king was also omitted, and the imposition of a penance of one year of waiting was, presumably, ascribed to a sense, on the part of the Princess, that it is expedient and will prove salutary. The pageant was transposed to the end of the comedy, which closed with one of the sweetest of the Shakespeare melodies and left its spectator with a mental vision of all the lovely flowers that grow on Avon's banks.

XIV.

SHAKESPEARE'S SHREW.

A PLAY entitled *The Taming of a Shrew* was published in London in 1594. It had been for some time extant and had been "sundry times" acted by the players who were in the service of the Earl of Pembroke. The authorship of it is unknown; but Charles Knight ascribes it to Robert Greene (1561–1592) — that dissolute genius, who is now chiefly remembered as the detractor of Shakespeare and as the first English poet that ever wrote for bread. The German commentator Tieck supposes it to be a juvenile production by Shakespeare himself; but this is a dubious theory. It is certain, however, that Shakespeare was acquainted with that piece, and it is believed that in writing *The Taming of the Shrew* he either co-laboured with another dramatist to make a new version of the older play, or else that he augmented and embellished a new version of it which

had already been made by another hand.
In 1594 he was thirty years old, and he
had been about eight years in London theatrical life. Edward Dowden thinks that
Shakespeare's portion of this task was
performed in 1597. *The Taming of the
Shrew* was acted, by his associates, at
the Blackfriars theatre, at the theatre at
Newington Butts — which the Shakespeare
players occupied while the Globe theatre
was being built — and finally at the Globe
itself. He never claimed it, however, as
one of his works, and it was not published
until after his death. It first appeared in
the folio of 1623.

Keightley describes *The Taming of the
Shrew* as "a rifacimento of an anonymous
play," and expresses the opinion that its
style "proves it to belong to Shakespeare's
early period." Collier maintains that
"Shakespeare had little to do with any
of the scenes in which Katherine and Petruchio are not engaged." Dr. Johnson,
comparing the Shakespearean play with its
predecessor, remarks that "the quarrel in
the choice of dresses is precisely the same;
many of the ideas are preserved without
alteration; the faults found with the *cap*,
the *gown*, the *compassed cape*, the *trunk*

sleeves, and the balderdash about *taking up the gown,* have been copied, as well as the scene in which Petruchio makes Katherine call the sun the moon. The joke of addressing an elderly gentleman as a ' young, budding virgin, fair and fresh and sweet,' belongs also to the old drama; but in this instance it is remarkable that, while the leading idea is adopted, the mode of expressing it is quite different."

Richard Grant White says : " The plot, the personages, and the scheme of the Induction are taken from the old play, which, however, is as dull as this is in most points spirited and interesting. In (this play) three hands at least are traceable ; that of the author of the old play, that of Shakespeare himself, and that of a co-labourer. The first appears in the structure of the plot and in the incidents and the dialogue of most of the minor scenes ; to the last must be assigned the greater part of the love business between Bianca and her two suitors ; while to Shakespeare himself belong the strong, clear characterisation, the delicious humour, and the rich verbal colouring of the recast Induction, and all the scenes in which Katherine, Petruchio, and Grumio are prominent figures, together

o

with the general effect produced by scattering lines and words and phrases here and there, and removing others elsewhere, throughout the play."

It is evident from these testimonies that, whether Shakespeare recast and rewrote his own work, — as Tieck supposes, and as he seems to have done in the case of *Hamlet*, — or whether he furbished up the work of somebody else, the comedy of *The Taming of the Shrew* that stands in his name is largely indebted, for structure, to its predecessor on the same subject. Both plays owe their plot to an ancient source. The scheme of the Induction — a feature common to both — is found as an old historic fact in *The Arabian Nights*, in the tale of *The Sleeper Awakened*. Shakespeare did not know that work ; but this tale of imposture — said to have been practised upon Abu-l-Hassan, "the wag," by the Khaleefeh Er-Rasheed — originating in remote oriental literature, and repeated in various forms, may have been current long before his time. In that narrative Abu-l-Hassan is deluded into the idea that he is the Prince of the Faithful, and, as that potentate, he commands that much gold shall be sent to Hassan's mother, and that punishment shall be inflicted upon certain persons by whom Hassan has been persecuted.

A variation of this theme occurs in Goulart's *Admirable and Memorable Histories*, translated into English by E. Grimestone, in 1607. In this it is related that Philip, Duke of Burgundy, called the Good, found a drunken man asleep in the street, at Brussels, caused him to be conveyed to the palace, bathed and dressed, entertained by the performance of "a pleasant comedy," and at last once more stupefied with wine, arrayed in ragged garments, and deposited where he had been discovered, there to awake, and to believe himself the sport of a dream. Malone, by whom the narrative was quoted from Goulart, thinks that it had appeared in English prior to the old play of *The Taming of a Shrew*, and consequently was known to Shakespeare.

Another source of his material is Ariosto. In 1587 were published the collected works of George Gascoigne. Among them is a prose comedy called *The Supposes* — a translation of Ariosto's *I Suppositi*, in which occur the names of Petrucio and Licio, and from which, doubtless, Shakespeare borrowed the amusing incident of the Pedant personating Vincentio. Gascoigne, it will

be remembered, is the old poet to whom Sir
Walter Scott was indebted, when he wrote
his magnificent novel of *Kenilworth* — so
superb in pageantry, so strong and various
in character, so deep and rich in passion,
and so fluent in style and narrative power
— for description of the revels with which
Leicester entertained Queen Elizabeth in
1575.

In versification the acknowledged Shakespearean comedy is much superior to the
older piece. The Induction contains passages of felicitous fluency, phrases of delightful aptness, that crystalline lucidity of style
which is characteristic of Shakespeare, and
a rich vein of humour. Those speeches
uttered by the Lord have the unmistakable
Shakespearean ring. The character of
Christopher Sly likewise is conceived and
drawn in precisely the vein of Shakespeare's usual English peasants. Hazlitt
justly likens him to Sancho Panza. The
Warwickshire allusions are also significant
— though Greene as well as Shakespeare
was a Warwickshire man ; but some of the
references are peculiar to the second comedy,
and they inevitably suggest the same hand
that wrote *The Merry Wives of Windsor*.
" Burton Heath " may be Barton-on-the-

Heath, a village situated about two miles from Long Compton. Knight, citing Dugdale, points out that in Doomsday-Book the name of this village is written "Bertone." Shakespeare's own beautiful native shire — as his works abundantly show — was constantly in his mind when he wrote. It is from the region round about Stratford-upon-Avon that he habitually derives his climate, his foliage, his flowers, his sylvan atmosphere, and his romantic and always effective correspondence between nature's environment and the characters and deeds of humanity. Only Sir Walter Scott, Wilkie Collins, and Thomas Hardy, since his time, have conspicuously rivalled him in this latter felicity; and only George Eliot and Thomas Hardy have drawn such English peasants as his. "Ask Marion Hacket, the fat ale-wife of Wincot," is another of the Warwickshire allusions; Wincot may mean Wilmcote — which Malone says was called Wyncote — where lived Mary Arden, the mother of Shakespeare, in that venerable, weather-beaten structure, in the parish of Aston Cantlow, about four miles northwest of Stratford. And there is a Wincot near the village of Clifford, a few miles to the south.

The version of *The Taming of the Shrew*
which for many years has been used on the
stage, in one form or another, is the version,
in three acts, that was made by Garrick,
produced at Drury Lane, and published in
1756, under the name of *Katherine and Petruchio*. That version omits several scenes
and transposes other parts of the original.
An alteration of Garrick's piece, made and
long used by Edwin Booth, was published
in 1878, with a preface and notes by the
present writer. Booth's version is in two
acts, and it has been adopted by several
other actors. Neither the Garrick nor the
Booth book includes The Induction or the
under-plot relative to the love of Hortensio
and Bianca. From the beginning of American stage history until the time of Augustin
Daly's revival of it, January 18, 1887, with
Ada Rehan in her superb and matchless
embodiment of Katherine, *The Taming
of the Shrew* had never been presented
here as Shakespeare wrote it. That exquisite actress Marie Seebach, when she
visited America in 1870, produced it, in the
German language, under the name of *Die
Widerspenstige*, in a four-act version, cut
and changed ; but that did not include the
Induction.

On the English stage this comedy has
been the parent of several popular plays.
Aside from its rattling fun the subject
itself seems to possess a particular interest for those Britons whose chief article
of faith is the subordination of woman
to man. Long ago it became a settled
principle of the common law of England
that a man may beat his wife with a stick
not thicker than his thumb. The duck-
ing stool — a chair affixed to the end of a
beam, which rested on a pivot, and so
arranged that the culprit, bound into it,
could be repeatedly soused in a pond or
river — was used in England, to punish
a scolding woman, as late as 1809. John
Taylor, the water-poet, counted sixty whip-
ping-posts within one mile of London, prior
to 1630, and it was not till 1791 that the
whipping of female vagrants was forbidden
by statute. The brank, a peculiar and
cruel kind of gag, formerly in common use,
has been employed to punish a certain sort
of women within the memory of persons
still alive. Thackeray's caustic ballad of
Damages Two Hundred Pounds affords an
instructive glimpse of the view that has
been taken, by British law, of masculine
severity toward women. It is not meant

that the gentlemen of England are tyranni-
cal and cruel in their treatment of the
women ; far from it ; but that the predomi-
nance of John Bull, in any question between
himself and Mrs. Bull, is a cardinal doctrine
of the English law, and that plays illustrative of the application of discipline to
rebellious women have found favour with
the English audience.

Sawney the Scot, by John Lacy, acted at
Drury Lane and published in 1698, is an
alteration of *The Taming of the Shrew* and
is not so good a play ; yet it had success.
Another play derived from this original is
The Cobbler of Preston, by Charles Johnson,
a two-act farce, acted at Drury Lane and
published in 1716. A piece, by Christopher
Bullock, having the same title, was acted
at the same time at Lincoln's Inn Fields.
Both seem to have been well received.
John Fletcher's *Rule a Wife and have a
Wife* (1640) is perhaps the most notable
type of the popular plays of this class. In
that piece Leon pretends meekness and
docility, in order to win Margarita, and
presently becomes imperative for the control of her. Garrick used to personate
Leon, in an alteration of the comedy attributed to his own hand. It is worthy of

note that Fletcher, whose views of women are somewhat stern and severe (he was the son of that Fletcher, Dean of Peterborough, who troubled the last moments of Mary Stuart by his importunate religious exhortations to her upon the scaffold at Fotheringay Castle), nevertheless wrote a sequel to *The Taming of the Shrew,* in which Petruchio reappears, Katherine being dead, with a new wife, by whom he is henpecked and subdued. This is entitled *The Woman's Prize, or the Tamer Tamed,* and it was printed in 1647. John Tobin's comedy of *The Honeymoon* (1805), based on ideas derived from Shakespeare, Fletcher, and Shirley, portrays a husband's conquest of his wife's affections by personal charm, irradiating manliness and firmness of character ; and this piece is deservedly held in esteem. Petruchio's method is to meet turbulence with still greater turbulence, remaining, however, entirely good-natured throughout the stormiest paroxysms of violence, till at last his boisterous, kindly, rough, sinewy vigour and clamorous tumult overwhelm Katherine and disgust her with the exaggerated image of her own faults.

The scene of the Induction is obviously

Warwickshire; that of the main action of the comedy at Padua, and at the country-house of Petruchio — who comes to Padua from Verona. The period indicated is the sixteenth century, about the year 1535. The time supposed to be occupied by the action is four days. The name of Shakespeare's shrew is *Katharina Minola*. The Induction presents the only opportunity that Shakespeare's works afford for showing English costume of his own time. The Italian dresses required for the piece are of styles such as were contemporaneous with the poet. An actor named Sincklo, who is mentioned in the quarto edition of *Henry IV.*, Part Second, and also in *Henry VI.*, Part Third, is supposed to have acted in *The Taming of the Shrew*, as well as in those two histories — for the reason that a reference to him occurs in the old play. The line "I think 'twas Soto that your honour means" was originally given to Sincklo. It has long been customary, in acting this piece, to present Curtis, a serving-man in the original, as an old woman; and to allot two or three words of speech to the servants who are named by Grumio, in his deprecatory appeal to his master, in the arrival scene.

XV.

A MAD WORLD: ANTONY AND CLEOPATRA.

WHATEVER else may be said as to the drift of the tragedy of *Antony and Cleopatra* this certainly may with truth be said, that to strong natures that sicken under the weight of convention and are weary with looking upon the littleness of human nature in its ordinary forms, it affords a great and splendid, howsoever temporary, relief and refreshment. The winds of power blow through it ; the strong meridian sunshine blazes over it ; the colours of morning burn around it ; the trumpet blares in its music ; and its fragrance is the scent of a wilderness of roses. Shakespeare's vast imagination was here loosed upon colossal images and imperial splendours.   The passions that clash or mingle in this piece are like the ocean surges — fierce, glittering, terrible, glorious. The theme is the ruin of a demigod.   The adjuncts are empires.   Wealth of every sort is poured forth with regal and limitless profusion. The language glows with a prodigal emotion and towers to a superb height of eloquence. It does not signify, as modifying the effect of all this tumult and glory, that the stern truth of mortal evanescence is suggested all the way and simply disclosed at last in a tragical wreck of honour, love, and life. While the pageant endures it endures in diamond light, and when it fades and crumbles the change is instantaneous to darkness and death.

> "The odds is gone,
> And there is nothing left remarkable
> Beneath the visiting moon."

There is no need to inquire whether Shakespeare — who closely followed Plutarch, in telling the Roman and Egyptian story — has been true to the historical fact. His characters declare themselves with absolute precision and they are not to be mistaken. Antony and Cleopatra are in middle life, and the only possible or admissible ideal of them is that which separates them at once and forever from the gentle, puny, experimental emotions of youth, and invests them with the developed powers and fearless and exultant pas-

sions of men and women to whom the
world and life are a fact and not a dream.
They do not palter. For them there is
but one hour, which is the present, and one
life, which they will entirely and absolutely
fulfil. They have passed out of the mere
instinctive life of the senses, into that more
intense and thrilling life wherein the senses
are fed and governed by the imagination.
Shakespeare has filled this wonderful play
with lines that tell unerringly his grand
meaning in this respect — lines that, to
Shakespearean scholars, are in the alphabet
of memory : —

"There's beggary in the love that can be reck-
    oned."

    . . . .

"There's not a minute of our lives should
    stretch
Without some pleasure now."

    . . . .

"Let Rome in Tiber melt and the wide arch
Of the ranged empire fall! Here is my
    space!"

    . . . .

"O, thou day of the world,
Chain mine armed neck! Leap thou, attire
    and all,

Through proof of harness, to my heart and
    there
Ride on the pants triumphant."
  . . . .

"Fall not a tear, I say! one of them rates
    All that is won and lost.   Give me a kiss;
    Even this repays me."

Here is no Orsino, sighing for the music
that is the food of love; no Romeo, taking
the measure of an unmade grave; no Hamlet lover, bidding his mistress go to a nunnery.   You may indeed, if you possess the
subtle, poetic sense, hear, through this
voluptuous story, the faint, far-off rustle of
the garments of the coming Nemesis; the
low moan of the funeral music that will
sing those imperial lovers to their rest —
for nothing is more inevitably doomed than
mortal delight in mortal love, and no moralist ever taught his lesson of truth with
more inexorable purpose than Shakespeare
uses here.   But in the meantime it is the
present vitality and not the moral implica-
tion of the subject that actors must be con-
cerned to show, and observers to recognise
and comprehend, upon the stage, if this
tragedy is to be rightly acted and rightly
seen.   Antony and Cleopatra are lovers,

but not lovers only. It is the splendid stature and infinite variety of character in them that render them puissant in fascination. Each of them speaks great thoughts in great language. Each displays noble imagination. Each becomes majestic in the hour of danger and pathetically heroic in the hour of death. The dying speeches of Antony are in the highest vein that Shakespeare ever reached ; and, when you consider what is implied as well as what is said, there is nowhere in him a more lofty line than Cleopatra's

"Give me my robe, put on my crown ; I have
    Immortal longings in me ! "

Antony at the last is a ruin, and like a ruin — dark, weird, grim, lonely, haggard — he seems to stand beneath a cold and lurid sunset sky, wherein the black clouds gather, while the rising wind blows merciless and terrible over an intervening waste of rock and desert. Those images indicate the spirit and atmosphere of Shakespeare's conception.

XVI.

SHERIDAN AND THE SCHOOL FOR SCANDAL.

ALTHOUGH genius is elemental, and therefore is not created by circumstances, it is certain that circumstances exert an important influence upon its drift and upon the channels and methods of its expression. Sheridan — whose father was an actor and whose mother was a dramatist, and who was born at Dublin in 1751, and trained at Harrow School from 1762 till 1769, when he went to reside with his father at Bath — came upon the scene at a period when English society was in an exceedingly artificial condition ; and this prevalent artificiality of manners, as experience subsequently proved, was destined to increase and to prevail during the whole of his career (he died in 1816), and not to decline until after the death of George IV. in 1830. When Sheridan went to reside at Bath he was in his nineteenth year ; a remarkably handsome youth ; ar-

dent and impressible ; and Bath was then
one of the gayest cities in the British kingdom. In that brilliant city and in that
opulent, insincere, tattling, backbiting society — intermittently, but most of the time
— he lived during the perilous years of his
youth, from 1770 to 1776 ; there he loved
and won for a wife the beautiful Eliza
Linley — eloping with her to France, and
fighting duels in her defence when he came
back ; there he wrote *The Rivals* and *The
Duenna*, and there he planned and partly
executed the *School for Scandal*. Into
The Rivals he wrought much of his personal experience, duly and artistically
modified and veiled. Into the *School for
Scandal* he wrought the results of his
observation — working in a manner essentially natural to his order of mind, yet one
that was to some extent guided and impelled by the study of Etherege, Wycherley, Farquhar, Vanbrugh, and Congreve,
who are his intellectual ancestors. There
is more freedom, more freshness of impulse, more kindness, more joy, more
nature in *The Rivals* than there is in the
School for Scandal ; but both are artificial ;
both reflect, in a mirror of artistic exaggeration, the hollow, feverish, ceremonious,

P

bespangled, glittering, heart-breaking fashionable world, in which their author's mind was developed and in which they were created. The *School for Scandal*, indeed, is completely saturated with artificiality, and the fact that it was intended to satirise and rebuke the faults of an insincere, scandal-mongering society does not — and was not meant to — modify that pervasive and predominant element of its character.

Satire, in order to be effective, must portray the thing that it excoriates. The *School for Scandal* rebukes a vice by depicting it, and makes the rebuke pungent by depicting it in a brilliant and entertaining way ; yet there is no considerable comedy in our language, not even one by Etherege or by Congreve [1] — authors whose

---

[1] The student of the comedies of Sheridan is aided in his appreciation of their quality, their spirit, their peculiar excellence, by a preliminary study of Etherege, Wycherley, Farquhar, Vanbrugh, and Congreve. The intellectual line represented by those writers closed with Sheridan. No successor has arisen, although of imitators there have been scores. Sir George Etherege (1636?–1689) wrote *The Comical Revenge* (1664), *She Would if She Could* (1668), and *The Man of Mode, or Sir Fopling Flutter* (1676). William Wycherley (1640–1715) wrote, between 1672 and 1677, *Love in a Wood*, *The Gentleman Dancing-Master*, *The Country*

influence was naturally and cogently oper-
ative upon the kindred mind of Sheridan —
that stands further off from the simplicity
of nature, moves in a more garish light, or
requires for its intelligible and effective
interpretation a more studied, manufac-
tured, fantastic manner.   It contains no
person upon whom the imagination can dwell
with delight, or to whom the heart can become devoted ; no person who either fires the
mind by example, or arouses the imagination by romantic nobility, or especially

Wife, and *The Plain-Dealer.* Moore found it difficult to believe that Sheridan was unfamiliar with the
last of these pieces; it is extremely probable that he
had a cursory knowledge of them all. George Farquhar (1678–1707) wrote *Love and a Bottle* (1699),
The Constant Couple (1700), *Sir Harry Wildair*
(1701), *The Inconstant* (1702), *The Twin Rivals*
(1703), *The Stage Coach* (1705), in which he was
assisted by Peter A. Motteux (1660–1718), *The Recruiting Officer* (1705), and *The Beaux Stratagem*
(1707). Sheridan had the same Irish grace that is
found in Farquhar, but he more closely resembles
Congreve in terseness and glitter. Sir John Vanbrugh (1666?–1726) wrote *The Relapse* (1697), *The
Provoked Wife* (1697), *Æsop* (1697), *The Pilgrim*
(1700), *The False Friend* (1702), *The Confederacy*
(1705), *The Mistake* (1706), *The Cuckold in Conceit*
(1706), *The Country House* (1715), and *A Journey
to London* (1728). *Squire Trelooby* (1734) is also attributed to him. Vanbrugh wrote with more appar-
ent facility than either of the others in this group,

wins esteem whether for worth of character
or excellence of conduct. Once or twice
indeed — as in Charles's impulsive expression of grateful sentiment toward the boun-
teous uncle whom he supposes to be absent
from the scene of the auction, and in Sir
Peter Teazle's disclosure to Joseph of his
considerate intentions toward his volatile
wife, in the scene of the screen — it imparts
a transient thrill of feeling. But it never
strikes — and, indeed, it never aims to
strike — the note of pathos, in its por-

---

and his language is more flexible, more like the language of actual men and women, than that of the
rest. William Congreve (1670-1729) wrote *The Old
Bachelor* (1693), *The Double-Dealer* (1694), *Love
for Love* (1695), *The Mourning Bride* (1697), *The
Way of the World* (1700), *The Judgment of Paris,
a Masque* (1701), and *Semele* (1707). Moore notes
the significant fact that the best comedies have
generally been written by young authors. All of
Congreve's pieces were written before he was
twenty-five. Farquhar died at thirty. Vanbrugh
began early. Sheridan at twenty-seven had written
The School for Scandal, and he never surpassed it;
indeed, practically, he wrote no more for the stage
— for *Pizarro* and *The Stranger* (which substantially are his) are scarcely worth remembrance.
But the reason why good comedies may be written
by clever young men is not obscure. Comedy must
necessarily treat of society and manners, and this
subject, which ceases to be interesting as men grow
old, is for youth a delightful inspiration.

traiture of human life ; so that, in the main, it contains scarcely a single trait of simple humanity. And yet its fascination is universal, indomitable, irresistible, final — the fascination of buoyant, intellectual character, invincible mirth, pungent satire, and a gorgeous affluence of polished wit. It succeeded when it was first produced, and now, after the lapse of a hundred years and more, it still continues to please, equally when it is acted and when it is read. There is a moral in this which ought to carry comfort to those votaries of art who believe in symbol rather than in fact, the ideal rather than the literal ; who know that a dramatic picture of life, in order that it may be made universal in its applicability and incessant in its influence, must be made to present aggregate and comprehensive personifications and not local and particular portraits, and must be painted in colours that are not simply true but delicately exaggerated. This is the great art — the art which has made Shakespeare to survive when Ben Jonson is dead. The absence of genial emotion — of the glow of expansive humanity and of pathos — in the *School for Scandal* is, perhaps, to be regretted ; but in this case a deficiency of

the melting heart is counterbalanced by a
prodigality of the opulent mind. The
piece transcends locality and epoch. The
resident not only of Bath and of London,
but of New York and San Francisco, the
denizen not only of great capitals but of
provincial villages, the inhabitant of yesterday, to-day, and to-morrow, can perceive
the meaning, feel the power, and rejoice in
the sparkling gayety of the *School for
Scandal*.

This great comedy — produced when its
author was in his twenty-seventh year —
was written slowly, painfully, and with
patient labour. Moore devotes about thirty
pages of his *Life of Sheridan* to an exposition of the two distinct sketches that the
dramatist first made, when rearing the
fabric of the piece, and dilates with particular admiration upon the scrupulous study,
the fastidious care, and the anxious severity
of revision with which he selected his language, moulded his materials, and blended
and fused the many scattered threads of
his fancy and inventive thought into one
symmetrical fabric of crystal wit. "Nothing great and durable," exclaims the delighted biographer (and Moore was a man
of excellent judgment, great reading, and a

beautiful faculty in literature), "has ever
been produced with ease. . . . Labour
is the parent of all the lasting wonders of
this world, whether a verse or stone,
whether poetry or pyramids." The original
manuscripts of the comedy manifested
especially to Moore's discerning eye "a
certain glare and coarseness," showing the
effect of recent study of Wycherley and
Vanbrugh; but also they revealed the
steady pressure of a delicate taste and the
incessant operation of strenuous refinement, alike in the improvement of the
characters, the conduct of the plot, the
formation and arrangement of the sentences,
and the choice of epithets. One of Sheridan's peculiarities, indeed, was a light,
graceful, indolent manner of elegant leisure.
He preferred that people should suppose
that his work was always done spontane-
ously and with careless ease. In reality he
accomplished nothing without effort. During a considerable part of his life — certainly till he was thirty-six, when he
joined Edmund Burke's sentimental crusade
against Warren Hastings and fortified the
rancorous rhetoric of that statesman by a
refulgent burst of verbal fireworks concerning the Begum Princesses of Oude — his

industry was minute, assiduous, and vigilant.
No man was ever a more pertinacious worker,
and no man ever seemed to have less occupation or less need of endeavour for the
accomplishment of splendid things.   He
did not, as so many fussy people do — who
cannot endure to be employed without an
everlasting fluster of cackle over the virtue of
their toil — intrude his labour upon the attention of his friends.   He displayed the finished
statue ; he did not vaunt the chips and the
dust that were made in the cutting of it.
He gave results ; he did not proclaim the
process of their production.   " Few persons with so much natural brilliancy of
talents," says Moore, " ever employed
more art and circumspection in their display."   But Sheridan's reticence in this
particular was not exclusively of a theatrical kind.   He held the most of human
achievements to be (as certainly they are)
of slight importance ; he shrunk with all
his soul from the disgrace and humiliation
of being a bore ; and he possessed in extraordinary fulness, and therefore he abundantly exerted, the rare faculty of taste.
There can be no doubt that, as time wore
on, the character of Sheridan was weakened
and degraded by misfortune, embarrass-

ment, profligate associations (with the Prince Regent and his shameless set), and most of all by intemperance; but at the beginning of his life, and for some years of his splendid productiveness and prosperity, he was a noble gentleman and a most individual mental power; and there is no reason why a virtue of his character should be set down to its weakness.

The *School for Scandal* was produced under auspicious circumstances. Garrick had read it and pronounced it excellent. Garrick, moreover, had assisted at its rehearsals, and had written a prologue to introduce it. Arthur Murphy, in his life of that great actor — then retired from the stage — says that Garrick was never known on any former occasion to be more anxious for a favourite piece. On the first night, May 8, 1777, the doors of Drury Lane theatre, which were opened at half-past five, had not been opened an hour when the house was crowded. The receipts that night were £225. King spoke the prologue, which is in Garrick's more whimsical and sprightly manner. Colman furnished an epilogue. The rehearsals had been numerous and careful. Sheridan, who was manager as well as author, had taken great

pains. Every part was well acted. The
incessant play of wit created an effect of
sparkling animation. Mrs. Abington, King,
and Smith — who played respectively Lady
Teazle, Sir Peter Teazle, and Charles Surface — were uncommonly brilliant. Palmer,
as Joseph Surface, was superb. The only
defect noticed was a sluggishness of movement in act second, incident to some excess
of talk by the clique of scandal-mongers.
Garrick observed that the characters upon
the stage at the falling of the screen waited
too long before they spoke. At the close
of the screen scene, nevertheless, ending
the fourth act, the applause was tremendous. Frederick Reynolds, the dramatist,
happening to pass through the pit passage,
"from Vinegar yard to Brydges street,"
about nine o'clock that night, heard such a
noise, all at once, that he thought the theatre was about to fall, and ran for his life.
The public enthusiasm, after the final
descent of the baize, was prodigious. Sheridan was so delighted that he quaffed un-
limited wine, got drunk, made a row in the
street, and was knocked down and put into
the watch-house. The London newspapers
teemed with praises of the comedy, not
only on the next day but on many days

thereafter. Horace Walpole, who speedily went to see it, wrote thus from his retreat at Strawberry Hill: "To my great surprise there were more parts performed admirably in this comedy than I almost ever saw in any play. Mrs. Abington was equal to the first in her profession. Yates, Parsons, Miss Pope, and Palmer, all shone." Boaden, the biographer, in allusion to King and Mrs. Abington as Sir Peter and Lady Teazle, said they were so suited to each other that they lost half their soul in separation. For years afterward the success of the *School for Scandal* was so great in London that it clouded the fortune of the new pieces that were brought forward in its wake. From the capital it went to Bath, Edinburgh, York, Dublin, and other large towns of the kingdom. Moore records that the scenes of the auction and the screen were presented upon the Paris stage in 1778, in a piece called *Les Deux Neveux*, and that the whole story soon found its way to the Théâtre Français, under the name of *Tartuffe de Mœurs*. Genest, commenting on the first cast, and speaking from his ample knowledge of the chronicles of the first performance (if not, possibly, from personal recollection), observes that "this comedy was so admirably acted that though it has continued on the acting list at Drury Lane from that time to this (1832), and been several times represented at Covent Garden and the Haymarket, yet no new performer has ever appeared in any one of the principal characters that was not inferior to the person who acted it originally." The statement is made in *The Thespian Dictionary* (1802), that "the copy of this play was lost after the first night's representation, and all the performers in it were summoned together early the next day in order, by the assistance of their parts, to prepare another prompter's book."

The London productions of the *School for Scandal* recorded by Genest[1] are these :

Drury Lane..................May 8, 1777.
Haymarket............September 2, 1785.
Drury Lane..................April 8, 1797.
Drury Lane..................May 18, 1798.
Covent Garden...........March 31, 1798.
Covent Garden............May 30, 1810.
Covent Garden...........March 23, 1813.
Covent Garden......September 10, 1818.
Drury Lane...........December 1, 1825.

[1] *Some Account of the English Stage,* from the Restoration in 1660 to 1830. In Ten Volumes. (By

It is more than half a century since the industrious, loquacious, sensible, matter-of-fact parson of Bath made up his chronicle, and many brilliant representations of the *School for Scandal* have been accomplished within that time on both sides of the Atlantic. The method in which the piece was originally acted, however, has been preserved by tradition, and actors in succeeding generations have seldom widely departed from it — although they may have fallen short of its reputed perfection (a point by no means certain). That method was the delicate, brilliant exaggeration of the manners of polite society in the days of George III. Mrs. Abington (1738–1815), the original representative of Lady Teazle, made her, radically and consistently, the affected fine lady, without giving the slightest indication that she had ever been "a girl bred wholly in the country"; and Mrs. Abington's example has usually, and perhaps involuntarily, been followed. Elizabeth Farren (1759–1829), who succeeded Mrs. Abington at Drury Lane, gave a remarkably elegant performance of the part,

the Rev. John Genest, of Bath.) Bath: Printed by H. E. Carrington. Sold by Thomas Rodd, Great Newport street, London, 1832.

harmonious as to artifice with the ideal indicated by her predecessor, but superior to
that ideal in natural refinement. It was in
this character that Miss Farren took leave
of the stage, April 8, 1797, just before her
marriage with the Earl of Derby.[1] The
next important embodiment of Lady Teazle
was that of Dora Jordan (1762-1816). That
delightful actress, while assuming the affected fine lady, allowed an occasional trace
of rustic breeding to show itself through an
artificial manner. John Galt, who wrote
biographies of both Miss Farren and Mrs.
Jordan, but had never seen either of them,
states that Dora Jordan's impersonation of
Lady Teazle was praised for "those little
points and sparkles of rusticity which are
still, by the philosophical critics, supposed
to mark the country education of the fascinating heroine." And Galt's parallel between the two is instructively significant.
Miss Farren was "as the camellia of the
conservatory — soft, beautiful, and deli-

---

[1] "I recollect the circumstance of seeing Lord
Derby leaving his private box to creep to her (Miss
Farren) behind the screen, and, of course, we all
looked with impatience for the discovery, hoping
the screen would fall a little too soon and show to
the audience Lord Derby as well as Lady Teazle."
— MISS WYNNE'S *Diary of a Lady of Quality.*

cate." Mrs. Jordan was "as the rose of the garden, sprinkled with dew." All the representatives of Lady Teazle, for a hundred years, have been one or the other of the varieties thus denoted.

Historic chronicles record many distinguished names of actors upon the British stage who have been identified with the *School for Scandal* and who have sharpened the outline and deepened the colour of those traditions as to its performance which it was a part of their vocation to transmit. King, who left the stage in 1802, had earlier parted from Sheridan. His immediate successors as Sir Peter Teazle were Richard Wroughton and the elder Mathews (1776–1835), but neither of them was conspicuously fine in it. Mathews played Sir Peter at twenty-eight. Munden (1758–1832) acted it, with Mrs. Abington as Lady Teazle, on March 31, 1789, in London. Before that time he had acted it in Dublin with Miss O'Neill as Lady Teazle; and he opened the season of 1816–17 with it, at the new Drury Lane (the old one was burned down on February 24, 1809). During his farewell engagement, October 1 to October 31, 1823, at Drury Lane, he played it twice — on the 18th and on the 25th.

His performance of Sir Peter was always admired for polished deportment, freedom from suspicion, and boundless confidence. "When an actor retires," said Charles Lamb, "how many worthy persons must perish with him! With Munden — Sir Peter Teazle must experience a shock; Sir Robert Bramble gives up the ghost; Crack ceases to breathe." The discrimination here suggested is significant: Sir Peter was in the second grade — not the first — of that great actor's achievements. It was in the first grade, however, of the achievements of his eminent successor, William Farren [1] (1786-1861), the best Lord Ogleby of this century, on the British stage, who, while

[1] On the occasion when William Farren made his first appearance upon the London stage, playing Sir Peter Teazle, the *School for Scandal* was interpreted by a remarkable group of actors. This performance occurred at Covent Garden (Harris, manager), on September 10, 1818; and this is a part of the cast:

Sir Peter Teazle	Mr. Farren.
Sir Oliver Surface	Mr. Terry.
Joseph Surface	Mr. Young.
Charles Surface	C. Kemble.
Crabtree	Mr. Blanchard.
Sir Benjamin Backbite	Mr. Liston.
Lady Teazle	Louisa Brunton.
Maria	Miss Foote.
Mrs. Candour	Mrs. Gibbs.

he lacked robust vigour for the impersonation of Sir Anthony Absolute and kindred
characters, possessed exactly the lace-ruffle-
and-diamond style essential for the expression of Sir Peter Teazle's refinement,
high-bred testiness, and amused, satirical
cynicism. No English actor since Farren
has been esteemed his equal in this character. The most notable performance of
Sir Peter that the English audience has
seen since Farren's day was, apparently,
that of Samuel Phelps (1797–1872). It is
thought to have lacked Farren's distinction
and his delicacy of mechanism and finish,
but it was accounted remarkable for the
qualities of force, sincerity, authority, and
restraint. William Farren, son of "old
Farren," performed Sir Peter Teazle, in a
revival of the *School for Scandal* which
was effected at the Vaudeville theatre, London, in 1872, and gained public favour and
critical admiration.

The character of Lady Teazle has had
many representatives on the British stage,
only a few of whom are now remembered.
Louisa Brunton, who became Countess of
Craven, and Miss Smithson (1800–1854),
who wedded with Berlioz, the composer,
were among the earliest followers in the

footsteps of Mrs. Abington, Miss Farren, and Mrs. Jordan. Mrs. Warner (1804–1854), acted the part with Phelps, and was esteemed one of its best representatives. Lucy Elizabeth Vestris (1798–1856) gave an impersonation of Lady Teazle, which, although superficial and shallow, was exceedingly vivacious and piquant. Louisa Cranstoun Nisbett (1812–1858), who became Lady Boothby — the most radiant and enchanting of the old stage beauties — made the part bewitching and brilliant, without suggestion of much sincerity or depth. One of the most highly esteemed and thoughtfully commended portrayals of Lady Teazle that have been recorded of late years was that given by Marie Wilton (Mrs. Bancroft) at the Prince of Wales theatre, London, in April 1874. That intellectual and polished actress Genevieve Ward has acted it, with sparkling effect, both in French and English.

The American record of the *School for Scandal* begins with a performance of it given at the John street theatre, New York, on December 16, 1785. The famous piece was then acted — according to the excellent authority of Ireland — "probably for the first time in America." The first representation that the comedy received at the old Park theatre occurred on December 3, 1798. Since then it has been performed in every considerable theatre in the United States, and often it has enlisted the talent of remarkably brilliant groups of actors. There is probably no veteran play-goer who could not, with slight effort of the memory, recall a cast of the *School for Scandal* which he would regard as incomparable and memorable. No piece has enjoyed more favour as the signalising feature of special dramatic occasions.[1] The chief part — the part that is a

---

[1] The comedy was acted, with this excellent cast, for the benefit of John Brougham, at Niblo's theatre, May 19, 1869, p.m.:

Sir Peter Teazle.....................John Gilbert.†
Sir Oliver Surface................John Brougham.†
Joseph Surface........................Neil Warner.
Charles Surface...................Edwin Adams.†
Crabtree............................A. W. Young.†
Sir Benjamin Backbite............Owen Marlowe.†
Rowley.................................T. J. Hind.†
Moses...............................Harry Beckett.†
Trip................................J. C. Williamson.
Snake...................................Frank Rae.†
Careless..............................J. W. Collier.
Sir Harry Bumper.......................R. Green.
Lady Teazle....................Mrs. D. P. Bowers.
Maria......................Miss Pauline Markham.
Lady Sneerwell................Mrs. John Sefton.†
Mrs. Candour.................Miss Fanny Morant.†

† Dead.

spring of crystal vitality for the whole fabric of the piece — is Lady Teazle, and upon the representative of that character the comedy is largely dependent. On the American stage Lady Teazle has been acted by Mrs. Morris, Mrs. Henry, Mrs. Hallam, Mrs. Lipman, Miss Westray (Mrs. W. B. Wood), Mrs. Shaw, Mrs. Gilfert, Fanny Kemble (September 21, 1832), Mrs. Hamblin, Miss Cooper, Rose Telbin, Sarah Anderton, Mrs. Russell (now Mrs. Hoey), Mme. Ponisi, Mrs. Mowatt, Catharine Sinclair (Mrs. Edwin Forrest), Ellen Tree (Mrs. Charles Kean), Julia Dean, Eliza Logan, Mrs. Catherine Farren, Jean Davenport (Mrs. Lander), Mrs. Bowers, Laura Keene, Miss Jane Coombs, Miss Madeline Henriques, Miss Rose Eytinge, Miss Fanny Davenport, Mrs. Julia Bennett Barrow, Mrs. Scott-Siddons, Miss Adelaide Neilson, Miss Rose Coghlan, Miss Augusta Dargon, Miss Annie Clarke, Mrs. F. B. Conway, Miss Ada Dyas, Mrs. Clara Jennings, Miss Ada Cavendish, Mrs. Rose Leland, Mrs. Langtry, and Miss Ada Rehan.

Among distinguished representatives of Sir Peter Teazle who have been seen on the American stage may be named Mr. Henry, Mr. Hallam, Mr. W. B. Wood, Joseph Jefferson, the grandfather of our Rip Van Winkle, William Warren (the father of the late William Warren, of our time, who also was famous and especially fine in this character), Mr. Twaits, Mr. Roberts, Mr. Blanchard, Mr. Finn, Mr. Chippendale, Henry Placide, Peter Richings, Henry Wallack, Charles Bass, William Rufus Blake, William Davidge, John Gilbert, Charles Fisher, Mark Smith, and Henry Edwards. The character of Charles Surface has been interpreted, for American audiences, by Mr. Hodgkinson, Mr. Cooper, George Barrett, Charles Kemble, Frederick B. Conway, James E. Murdoch, William Wheatley, George Vandenhoff, E. L. Davenport, Lester Wallack, Charles Wyndham, H. J. Montague, Osmund Tearle, Charles Coghlan, Charles Barron, George Clarke, and John Drew.

Most of the old comedies contain improprieties; sometimes of situation, more commonly of language; and those are not adornments but blemishes. Every old comedy, furthermore, which has survived in actual representation, has gathered to itself, in the course of years, a considerable number of extraneous passages, which may collectively, though perhaps not quite accu-

rately, be described as "gags." Those are
the contributions, mainly, of actors and
stage-managers. They are either figments
of fancy, or readily appreciable jokes, or
local and particular allusions, which, in
actual performance of the piece, were found
to be effective. In some cases they have
become so solidly incorporated into the
original text that they have gained acceptance as actually parts of the original structure, and the omission of them has been
known to prompt a righteous remonstrance
against the iniquity of tampering with the
author. As a rule they are both spoken
and heard under the impression that they
belong to the play. The "pickled elephant" that figures in Valentine's mad
scene, in *Love for Love*, might be cited as
an example of this sort of embellishment.
The passage is not in Congreve's text, but
it is generally used. It was introduced by
the elder Wallack — then a young man on
the London stage — on a night when he was
acting Valentine, in place of Elliston, who
was disabled with gout. That day an elephant had gone mad and been shot by the
guards, and this incident had caused much
popular excitement. Valentine, who is
pretending to be deranged, has to talk

wildly, and Wallack's sudden ejaculation, "Bring me a pickled elephant," was thought to be excellent lunacy — for it was received with copious applause ; and Elliston, seated in his invalid-chair, at the wing, accosted Wallack, as that actor came off, and mournfully exclaimed, "They never shot an elephant for me, young man !" Since then every representative of Valentine makes this allusion, although now the reference is pointless and the image stands in the category of Oriana's "tall, gigantic sights" and Tilburina's "whistling moon." The presence of such points in those old plays may well intimate to the judicious observer that their text has not, from the beginning, been regarded as a sacred thing, and that the prime necessity of the stage — which is effect — may sometimes be found to warrant both additions and omissions in the presentment of works that are, in some measure, obsolete. One thing is certain — that the indelicacy of those old pieces is offensive to the taste of the present time, and ought not ever, in these days, to be thrust upon an audience. It is not an answer to talk of "Bowdlerism," or to sneer at "purists," or to stigmatise refinement as squeamish folly. There is much pure gold in the old English comedy; but the dirt that is in it should be cast aside. Nor is the modern theatre under any sort of obligation to treat that body of stage literature as if it were a celestial revelation. The book of the *School for Scandal* prepared by Augustin Daly (who first produced the comedy at his theatre on September 12, 1874, and revived it on January 20, 1891, with Ada Rehan as Lady Teazle), has been edited in a spirit harmonious with these views. The coarseness of the scandal-mongering colloquies has been expunged. A few sentences have been dropped, in order to shorten the piece, and a few others have been transposed — the objects sought being incessant movement and the circumscription of each act within a single scenic picture. That comedy is not only the best work of one of the most brilliant writers that ever lived, but it is one of the best dramatic pieces ever written, and the revival of it from time to time will, doubtless, continue to occur upon the stage as long as the stage endures. This certainly should be hoped, for the *School for Scandal* teaches charity and reticence; and these are among the best virtues that adorn character and sanctify life.

XVII.

FARQUHAR AND THE INCONSTANT.

THE plays that survive from the past are the plays that are not, in their spirit, their character, their essential vitality, restricted to the particular fashion of the periods in which they were written. Jonson and Shakespeare lived and wrote side by side ; but while Jonson's plays are no longer acted those of Shakespeare still keep the stage. *The Alchymist* would not be accepted now, except, perhaps, for a night or two, by an audience of scholars and as a curiosity. That comedy contains, indeed, in the character of old Mammon, the dramatic ancestor of Sir Sampson Legend and Sir Anthony Absolute, and some of the speeches in it are wonderfully vigorous, ornate, and eloquent. Its object, however, was satire of a local and contemporaneous mania — the practice of astrology and the quest for the wonderful philosopher's stone that would transmute worthless metals into gold — and with the disappearance of that mania disappeared also the vitality of the satire upon it. *As You Like It*, on the other hand, and *Much Ado About Nothing*, because they are comedies dealing faithfully and powerfully with the elemental facts of human nature, are as much alive to-day, and as significant and welcome upon the stage as they were when first presented in Shakespeare's time. The dramatic author who portrays representative types of humanity rather than the ephemeral eccentricities of the hour in which he lives is recognised by mankind, in all periods, as being the bearer of a significant and interesting message. Farquhar, to some extent, dealt with the permanent and abiding facts of human nature, and that is one reason why he survives as a dramatist and pleases the public of to-day. The auxiliary reasons are his abundant flow of animal spirits, his droll humour, his nimble invention, his skill in raillery, and his graceful art in making sprightly language the spontaneous expression of gallant, mirthful, amorous, adventurous character — women who fascinate by every dazzling and melting charm of coquetry, and men who turn all life to a feast of roses and revel in its fragrance.

George Farquhar was born in 1678, at Londonderry, Ireland, and was educated at that place and at Trinity College, Dublin. He was the son of a clergyman and he proved to be a wild youth. He was entered at Trinity, as "a sizar," on July 17, 1694, and he left it in 1695. In college he was considered a dull fellow, and one account of him says that he was expelled for an irreverent jest, relative to one of the miracles recited in the New Testament ; while another relates that he left the university on account of the death of his patron, Dr. Wiseman, Bishop of Dromore. On leaving college he joined the Dublin theatre, then managed by Ashbury, and made his first appearance as an actor, choosing the part of Othello. That was in 1695. He remained on the stage only one season. His memory was strong, his delivery fluent, his demeanour elegant, his person good ; but his voice was feeble and he could never quite control a nervous tendency to stage fright. The immediate cause of his retirement from the stage, however, was an accident. He had the misfortune to inflict a dangerous wound upon a stage antagonist, when acting in Dryden's play of *The Indian Emperor,* and the thought that he had come near killing a fellow-creature so impressed his mind that he resolved to quit forever the profession of an actor. Such is the story ; but this sensitive disposition did not prevent him from becoming, subsequently, a soldier. He left Dublin, for London, in 1696, in the society of that brilliant actor Robert Wilks, and on reaching the capital of the British kingdom he speedily made a pleasant impression in society, and presently was fortunate enough to win the favour of the Earl of Orrery, who made him a lieutenant in his own regiment and sent him, on service, into Ireland and elsewhere, so that for several years he led a military life ; and it is recorded that he was invariably upright in his conduct and noted for his courage.

Wilks, who early discerned Farquhar's talent and perceived the drift of his mind, urged him to write for the stage, and in 1698 was brought out his first comedy — made in compliance with the wish of that good friend — *Love and a Bottle.* He afterward wrote *The Constant Couple, or a Trip to the Jubilee ; Sir Harry Wildair ; The Inconstant, or the Way to Win Him ; The Twin Rivals ; The Stage Coach ; The Recruiting Officer ;* and *The Beaux' Strata-*

gem. In *The Constant Couple* the character of Sir Harry Wildair first occurs — a part in which Wilks was conspicuously brilliant and which came to be intimately associated with the shining name of Peg Woffington. Wilks acted in every one of his plays and Anne Oldfield in two of them. *The Twin Rivals* was long regarded as Farquhar's most artistic composition, but it has not survived in equal repute with *The Inconstant* or *The Recruiting Officer*, or even *The Beaux' Stratagem ;* for the first two of those pieces are still acted, and the last, on account of the dashing character of Archer, long kept its place upon the stage, even in the theatre of America. *The Recruiting Officer*, it will be remembered, contains the sprightly part of Captain Plume and is a comedy of piquant reminiscence of Farquhar's own experience and observation while on duty in the romantic old city of Shrewsbury. It was the habit of this author to sketch himself in his wild, gallant characters, and he has aptly indicated his ideal of the bright original, in a string of expressive adjectives descriptive of Young Mirabel, whom he indicates, in the preface to *The Inconstant*, as " a gay, splendid, generous, easy, fine young gentleman."

Farquhar had a short life but a merry one,
notwithstanding that his temperament was
melancholy and his final experience unfortunate. It was he who discovered and first
recognised the talent of Anne Oldfield,
whom he found in the Mitre Tavern, in St.
James's Market; and it was under his
influence and that of Sir John Vanbrugh
that this brilliant girl was introduced upon
the stage, in 1699, by Rich, at the King's
theatre. Anne was only sixteen and Farquhar only twenty-one at that time, and
for a while they were lovers; but in 1703
the gentleman got married, and four years
later, in April 1707, he died — aged twenty-
nine. The marriage was a mercenary one,
on his part, and he appears to have been
properly rewarded by finding that his wife
had no fortune whatever. It is recorded,
though, that he took the disappointment
in a philosophical spirit and treated his
connubial partner with all possible chivalry.
Toward the last he sold his military com-
mission, in order to pay his debts, and
presently sunk into despondency and death.
His final effort was *The Beaux' Stratagem.*
His mental brilliancy and sportive humour
remained active and salient to the last.
When he was dead Wilks found among his

papers a forlorn little note which sadly and simply said : "Dear Bob, I have not anything to leave thee to perpetuate my memory but two helpless girls : Look upon them sometimes and think of him that was, to the last moment of his life, thine, George Farquhar."

The story of this brief and bright life seems a fit prelude to the sparkling play of *The Inconstant*, in which it is easy to perceive the author's ideal of himself, together with the essential characteristics of his mind and temperament. That piece, like all his works, has to be cut and altered a little, in order that it may be represented, for he did not scruple sometimes to write in a licentious vein and to use expressions which in these days would offend the audience. It is surprising, however, to consider how well that comedy bears being freed from the taint of sensual warmth, which was the characteristic of the plays of Farquhar's period, and how much excellent substance remains. Mirabel is the type of many young fellows who may be met with in society everywhere. He rejoices in his youth and strength, in gallantry and adventure, and he will keep his freedom. He loves Oriana, but having been contracted

to her he shrinks from matrimony. The
course of events is too methodical. Conventionality makes it insipid, and therefore
he breaks away and is inconstant. Such a
temperament inclines to value not what it
can have but what is denied to it; yet
presently it can be awakened by peril and
touched by devotion and made to realise
that life and love are very serious matters.
Oriana, devotedly fond of him, but likewise
skilful in coquetry, employs various wiles
in order to subdue this errant cavalier, and
the movement of the piece is the rapid and
continually shifting encounter of their wits,
in those stratagems of love. The flow of
intrigue, the variety of incident, the sparkle
of language, the undercurrent of passion,
the reality, sincerity, and piquancy of character, the occasional touches of sentiment,
the flexibility of action, and the absorbing
interest of the climax — at which a feeling
of almost agonised suspense is sustained
with superb skill — are living virtues in a
play ; and they make this one as significant
and valuable and enjoyable to the world
now as it was in the romantic days of good
Queen Anne. The closing scene of it,
which has always been much admired, is
said to have been partly based upon an in-

cident in the experience of the author. The
entire piece is founded on *The Wild Goose
Chase*, written by John Fletcher and produced in 1621. "I took the hint," says Farquhar, in his preface, "from Fletcher's *Wild
Goose Chase*, and to those who say that I
have spoiled the original I wish no other injury but that they would say it again."
Something more than a hint was, in fact,
taken from the elder dramatist; yet *The
Inconstant* contains much that is original,
and especially it lives and glows with the
characteristic spirit of impulsive, impetuous
sprightliness and wanton mirth which was
essentially Farquhar's nature. When first
produced this comedy was encumbered with
a miserable prologue of thirty-four lines,
written by P. A. Motteux and crammed full
of similes drawn from the cook's kitchen.
Also it was furnished with an epilogue by
the poet laureate, Nicholas Rowe, announc-
ing the moral of the piece to be that

" With easy freedom and a gay address
   A pressing lover seldom wants success,
   Whilst the respectful, like the Greeks, sits
      down,
   And wastes a ten years' siege before one
      town."

The Inconstant made its advent upon the

American stage on January 1, 1759, at the old theatre on Cruger's Wharf, New York. In June 1795 a three-act version of it, made by the reigning favourite Hodgkinson, was produced at the theatre in John street, with Hodgkinson as young Mirabel. In 1829 this old comedy was given at the Park theatre, and Mirabel was acted by George Barrett. In 1832, at the same theatre, the piece was represented with a distinguished cast of the characters, including Charles Kemble as young Mirabel, Henry Placide as old Mirabel, Mr. Simpson as Duretete, Mrs. Sharp as Oriana, and Fanny Kemble as Bisarre. Murdock first acted young Mirabel in New York in 1857 at Burton's theatre. Neither of the Wallacks appears to have played Mirabel, although Lester Wallack played Duretete. Among the representatives of Mirabel, in old times, were Gifford, 1744; Palmer, 1751; Smith, 1753; Wrougton, 1779; Farren, 1780; Pope, 1787; C. Kemble, 1811; and Rae, 1817. Those performances occurred at Drury Lane or Covent Garden, in London. Garrick, at Goodman's Fields, played Duretete, and this performance he repeated, for Kitty Clive's benefit, at Drury Lane, in 1761. The younger Bannister took Duretete in

1798. Oriana has been acted, among others, by Peg Woffington, the pretty Mrs. Davies, wife of Dr. Johnson's friend the actor and bookseller, Mrs. Lessingham, and Sally Booth. Kitty Clive played Bisarre, and so did Mrs. Abington.

Augustin Daly, who revived the comedy on November 7, 1872, with Clara Morris as Oriana, and again on January 8, 1889, with Ada Rehan in that character, pruned the text of *The Inconstant*, discarded the scene of the monkish masquerade, restored the passage portraying Duretete's rage and comic pugnacity at the end of act third, and compressed the piece into four acts; and at the latest of these revivals, a few lines by the present writer were added, by way of epilogue, spoken by Oriana — who ends the play.[1]   The custom of naming this piece

[1] Not yet! for what if Oriana choose
The crown of all your rapture to refuse?
Through many a maze of frolic, yet of pain,
Her faithful heart has felt your gay disdain.
Shall she not triumph, — now the strife is o'er —
And punish him who vexed her so before?
No! Take her hand: her heart has long been yours.
True love in trouble all the more endures!
She'll cling the closer for the risk she braved,
And cherish all the more the life she saved.
There's nought a loving woman will not do
When once she feels her lover's heart is true.

Wine Works Wonders (in allusion to the incident of the red Burgundy marked one thousand, in the last scene) originated many years ago, but that title was unknown to the time of Farquhar. Mirabel has been played by many dashing light comedians of the last hundred years and more, but upon the American stage the part is inseparably entwined with the name and fame of that glittering comedian of other days, James E. Murdoch. The serious side of Mirabel's nature was made earnest and sweet by him, and by establishing a conviction of his inherent manliness and generosity he intensified enjoyment of his superficial insincerity and his manifold pranks. Clara Morris, playing Oriana, presented a delicious type of womanhood, rich, variable, capricious, and by the simulation of beauty in piteous wreck, by sweet tenderness of voice, and by rapid alternations of tender and lightsome mood she made a deep impression. *The Inconstant* is one of those fanciful pieces that are entitled to be viewed through a haze of unreality, which makes ideal pictures grateful to the mind and which allows an innocent forgetfulness of the moralities.

XVIII.

LONGFELLOW.[1]

THE death of Longfellow comes home to hundreds of hearts with a sense of personal loss and bereavement. The lovable quality in his writings, which was the natural and spontaneous reflex of the gentleness of his nature, had endeared him not less as a man than as a poet. To read him was to know him, and, as Halleck said of Drake, to know him was to love him; so that his readers were his affectionate friends. The reading of Longfellow is like sitting by the fireside of a sympathetic and cherished companion. The atmosphere of his works has the refinement and elegance of a sumptuous, well-ordered library; but also it has the soft tranquillity and smiling contentment of a happy home.

To any one who ever was privileged to

[1] The poet Longfellow died on March 24, 1882. This paper was first published at that time.

sit by the fireside of the poet, the thought
of his death is almost inconceivable, and
it brings an overwhelming solemnity. No
man ever diffused a more radiant influence
of life, cheerfulness, and vigorous hope
than Longfellow did, beneath his own
roof. He was not, indeed, a demonstrative
person ; he did not overflow with effusion
or cover by a boisterous heartiness the absence of a sincere welcome. But he never
failed to do the right thing in the right way,
or to say the right word at the right time.
He was thoughtful for every one who ap-
proached him. He knew by unerring intuition the ways of true grace — which flow
out of true kindness. He was entirely frank
and simple, bearing himself always with
gentle dignity and speaking always with a
sweetness that was inexpressibly winning.
With youth in particular he had a profound
and comprehensive sympathy. He understood all its ardours and aspirations, its
perplexity in presence of the mysteries of
life, its embarrassment amid unfamiliar
surroundings, its craving for recognition,
its sensitive heart, and its dream-like spirit.
": The thoughts of youth are long, long
thoughts." To the last day of his life he
carried that mood of youth ; and no one

ever heard from his lips a word of satire or discouragement. His first and greatest impulse was sympathy. In domestic life this displayed itself in a constant, unobtrusive solicitude for the comfort of those around him, and in a thousand courtesies that equally adorned his conduct and comforted his associates. In his writings it is the lambent flame of every page.

Yet there was no element of insipidity in his character. If he preferred always to see the most agreeable side and to speak always the most agreeable word it was not that he was blind to defects, or assiduous to please, or insincere, or acquisitive of popularity. When occasion required it he spoke his convictions, whether acceptable or otherwise, fully and firmly, and he could rebuke injustice or ill-breeding with a cool censure that was all the more implacable for its calmness and reserve. He never obtruded his scholarship, but if the drift of conversation carried him that way he tinted his discourse with many a shining ray of knowledge and many a coloured flash of anecdote, with citations from a wide range of books, and with a peculiar, dry, half-veiled drollery that was kindly, mischievous, and delightfully pungent. His tolerance was neither a weakness nor an artifice; it was the outgrowth of constitutional charity and tenderness toward that human nature of which he possessed so much and which he knew so well.

Those who remember him in early years say that he was remarkable for personal beauty and for the order and refinement of his life and manners. From the first he seems to have possessed the composure of high poetic genius. Those who think that he was passionless and that he knew little or nothing of tragedy must have read to but little purpose such poems as *The Goblet of Life*, *The Light of Stars*, or the closing chapters of *Hyperion*. Even his familiar ballad of *The Bridge* is eloquent of a profound knowledge of grief; and it may be doubted whether our language contains a more absolute poetic note of anguish and fortitude — when one considers its bleak isolation and its mournful significance — than his lines called *Weariness*. He was not a Byron. His poetry is not the poetry of storm and stress. The "banner, torn but flying," that "streams like a thunderstorm against the wind," is nowhere unfurled in all his writings. But if he did not utter the conflict he clearly and sweetly

uttered the consciousness of it and the
grand clarion note of patience and conquest.
Of the trials and cares that are common to
humanity and that can be named and known
he had his share ; but also he had the experience which the poetic nature invariably
and inevitably draws upon itself. He had
felt all that Burns felt, in writing *To Mary
in Heaven*. He had felt all that Goethe
felt, in writing that wonderful passage of
Faust which ends with the curse on patience as the worst of human afflictions.
But he would suffer no shock of sorrow to
turn his life into a delirium. He would
meet every trouble as a man ought to meet
it who believes in the immortal destiny of
the human soul. When he lost, under circumstances so pathetic and tragical (1861),
the wife whom he so entirely loved (that
beautiful and stately lady, whom to remember is to wonder that so much loveliness
and worth could take a mortal shape), he
took the terrible anguish into the silent
chambers of his heart, he bore it with un-
flinching, uncomplaining fortitude ; and
from that day onward no reader of his
writings was visited with one repining murmur, one plea for sympathy, one wail of
personal loneliness or despondency or mis-

anthropical bitterness. All that was ever shown of that misery was the simple grandeur of endurance combined with even a more wistful and readier and deeper sympathy with the sorrows of mankind.

There are poets, and good ones too, who seem never to get beyond the necessity of utterance for their own sake. Longfellow was not an egotist. He thought of others; and the permanent value of his writings consists in this — that he helped to utter the emotions of the universal human heart. It is when a writer speaks for us what were else unspoken — setting our minds free and giving us strength to meet the cares of life and the hour of death — that he first becomes of real value. Longfellow has done this for thousands of human beings, and done it in that language of perfect simplicity — never bald, never insipid, never failing to exalt the subject — which is at once the most beautiful and the most difficult of all the elements of literature. And the high thoughts and tender feelings that he has thus spoken, the limpid, soft, and tranquil strain of his music — breathing out so truly our home loves, our tender longing for those that are dead and gone, the trust that we all would cherish in a happy future be-

yond the grave, the purpose to work nobly
and endure bravely while we live — will
sound on in the ears of the world, long
after every hand and heart that honours
him or grieves for him now is mouldering in
the dust.

The least of us who have recollections of
Longfellow may venture to add them to
the general stock of knowledge, without
incurring the reproach of intrusiveness.
I saw him often, long before I was honoured with his personal acquaintance ; and
I observed him closely — as a youth naturally observes the object of his honest
admiration. His dignity and grace and
the beautiful refinement of his countenance, together with his perfect taste in
dress and the exquisite simplicity of his
manners, made him the ideal of what a poet
should be. His voice was soft, sweet, and
musical, and, like his face, it had the innate
charm of tranquillity. His eyes were blue-
gray, very bright and brave, changeable
under the influence of emotion (as, afterward, I often saw), but mostly calm, attentive, and gentle. The habitual expression
of his face was not that of sadness ; yet it
was pensive. Perhaps it may be best described as that of serious and tender

thoughtfulness. He had conquered his own
sorrows, thus far, but the sorrows of others
threw their shadow over him — as he
sweetly and humanly says in his pathetic
ballad of *The Bridge*.

It was in April 1854 that I became personally acquainted with Longfellow, and he
was the first literary friend I ever had —
greeting me as a young aspirant in literature and holding out to me the hand of fel-
lowship and encouragement. He allowed
me to dedicate to him a volume of my
verses, published in that year, being the
first of my ventures. They were juvenile,
crude verses; yet he was tolerant of them,
because he knew that sincerity of heart and
ambition of spirit lay beneath them, and,
in his far-reaching charity and prescience,
he must have thought that something good
might come of even such a poor beginning.
At all events, where others were cold, or
satirical, or contemptuous, he was kind,
cordial, and full of cheer. A few words in
commendation of the book had been written by N. P. Willis and the paragraph happened to come in his way. He was pleased
with it, and I can hear now the earnest tone
in which he spoke of it, turning to Mrs.
Longfellow, who was present, and saying,

with an obvious relish of good-will: "There is much kindness in Willis's nature." This was a slight trait, but it is of little traits that the greatest human character is composed. Goodness, generosity, and a large liberality of judgment were, in his character, conspicuous elements. His spontaneous desire — the natural instinct of his great heart and philosophic mind — was to be helpful: to lift up the lowly; to strengthen the weak; to develop the best in every person; to dry every tear and make every pathway smooth. It is saying but little to say that he never spoke a harsh word except against injustice and wrong. He was the natural friend and earnest advocate of every good cause and right idea. His words about the absent were always considerate and he never lost a practical opportunity of doing good.

For the infirmities of humanity he was charity itself and he shrank from harshness as from a positive sin. "It is the prerogative of the poet," he once said to me, in those old days, "to give pleasure; but it is the critic's province to give pain." He had, indeed, but a slender esteem for the critic's province. Yet his tolerant nature found excuses for even as virulent and hos-

tile a critic as his assailant and traducer
Edgar Poe — of whom I have heard him
speak with genuine pity. His words were
few and unobtrusive and they clearly indicated his consciousness that Poe had
abused and maligned him; but instead of
resentment for injury they displayed only
sorrow for an unfortunate, distempered
adversary. There was a volume of Poe's
poems, an English edition, on the library
table, and at sight of this I was prompted
to ask Longfellow if Poe had ever personally met him — "because," I said, "if he
had known you it is impossible he could
have written about you in such a manner."
He answered that he had never seen Poe,
and that the bitterness was, doubtless, due
to a deplorable literary jealousy. Then,
after a pause of musing, he added, very
gravely: "My works seemed to give him
much trouble, first and last; but Mr. Poe
is dead and gone and I am alive and still
writing — and that is the end of the matter.
I never condescended to answer Mr. Poe's
attacks; and I would advise you now, at
the outset of your literary life, never to
take notice of any attacks that may be
made upon you. Let them all pass." He
then took up the volume of Poe, and, turn-

ing the leaves, particularly commended the
stanzas entitled *For Annie* and *The
Haunted Palace*. Then, still speaking of
criticism, he mentioned the great number
of newspaper and magazine articles, about
his own writings, that were received by
him — sent, apparently, by their writers.
" I look at the first few lines," he said,
" and if I find that the article has been
written in a pleasant spirit, I read it
through ; but if I find that the intention is
to wound, I drop the paper into my fire,
and so dismiss it. In that way one escapes
much annoyance."

Longfellow liked to talk of young poets,
and he had an equally humorous and kind
way of noticing the foibles of the literary
character. Standing in the porch, one summer day, and observing the elms in front of
his house, he recalled a visit made to him,
long before, by one of the many bards, now
extinct, who are embalmed in Griswold.
Then suddenly assuming a burly, martial
air, he seemed to reproduce the exact figure
and manner of the youthful enthusiast —
who had tossed back his long hair, gazed
approvingly on the elms, and in a deep
voice exclaimed, " I see, Mr. Longfellow,
that you have many trees — I love trees ! ! "

"It was," said the poet, "as if he gave a
certificate to all the neighbouring vegetation." A few words like these, said in
Longfellow's peculiar, dry, humorous manner, with a twinkle of the eye and a droll
inflection of the voice, had a charm of
mirth that was delightful. It was that
same demure playfulness which led him
to write of the lady who wore flowers
"on the congregation side of her bonnet,"
or to extol those broad, magnificent western roads which "dwindle to a squirrel-
track and run up a tree." He had no
particle of the acidity of biting wit; but he
had abundant, playful humour, that was
full of kindness and that toyed good-
naturedly with the trifles of life. That
such a sense of fun should be amused by
the ludicrous peculiarities of a juvenile bard
was inevitable.

I recall many talks with him, about
poetry, the avenues of literary labour, and
the discipline of the mind in youth. His
counsel was conveyed in two words — calmness and patience. He did not believe in
seeking experience or in going to meet bur-
dens. "What you desire will come, if you
will but wait for it" — that he said to me
again and again. "My ambition once was,"

he remarked, "to edit a magazine. Since
then the opportunity has been offered to
me many times — and I did not take it, and
would not." That same night he spoke of
his first poem — the first that ever was
printed — and described his trepidation
when going, in the evening, to drop the
precious manuscript into the editor's box.
This was at a newspaper office in Portland,
Maine, when he was a boy. Publication
day arrived and the paper appeared — but
not a word of the poem. "But I had another copy," he said, "and I immediately
sent it to the rival paper, and it was published." And then he described his exultation and inexpressible joy and pride,
when, — having bought a copy of the paper,
still damp from the press, and walked with
it into a by-street of the town, — he saw,
for the first time, a poem of his own actually in print! "I have never since had
such a thrill of delight," he said, "over
any of my publications."

His sense of humour found especial
pleasure in the inappropriate words that
were sometimes said to him by persons
whose design it was to be complimentary,
and he would relate, with a keen relish of
their pleasantry, anecdotes, to illustrate

this form of social blunder. Years ago he told me, at Cambridge, about a strange gentleman who was led up to him and introduced, at Newport, and who straightway said, with enthusiastic fervour, — "Mr. Longfellow, I have long desired the honour of knowing you! Sir, I am one of the few men who have read your *Evangeline*." Another of his favourites was related to me a day or two after it occurred. The writer's rule was to reserve the morning for work, and visitors were not received before noon. One morning a man forced his way past the servant who had opened the hall-door, and, going into the presence of the astonished author, in his library, addressed him in the following remarkable words: "Mr. Longfellow, you're a poet, I believe, and I've called here to see if I couldn't git you to write some poetry, for me to have printed, and stuck onto my medicine bottles. You see, I go round sellin' this medicine, and if you give me the poetry I'll give you a bottle of the carminative — and it's one dollar a bottle." For the enjoyment of that story it was needful to see the poet's face and hear the bland tone of his voice. Many years ago he told me that incident — sitting by the wide fire-place in the library back of his study. As I write his words now the wind seems again to be moaning in the chimney and the fire-light flickers upon his pale, handsome, happy face, and already silvered hair. He took delight in any bit of fun like that. He was always gracious, always kind, always wishful to make every one happy that came near him.

About poetry he talked with the earnestness of a genuine passion and yet with no particle of self-assertion. Tennyson's *Princess* was a new book when first I heard him speak of it, and I remember Mrs. Longfellow sitting with that volume in her hands and reading it by the evening lamp. The delicate loveliness of the lyrical pieces that are interspersed throughout its text was, in particular, dwelt upon as a supreme merit. Among his own poems his favourite at that time was *Evangeline ;* but he said that the style of versification which pleased him best was that of *The Day is Done ;* nor do I wonder, reading this now, together with *The Bridge, Twilight, The Children's Hour*, and *The Open Window*, and finding them so exquisite both in pathos and music. He said also that he sometimes wrote poems that were for himself alone, that he should not care to publish, because they were too delicate for publication. One of his sayings was that "the desire of the young poet is not for applause but for recognition." He much commended the example, in one respect, of the Italian poet Alfieri, who caused himself to be bound into his library chair and left for a certain period of time, each day, at his library table — his servants being strictly enjoined not to release him till that time had passed : by this means he forced himself to labour. No man ever believed more firmly than Longfellow did in regular, proportioned, resolute, incessant industry. His poem of *The Builders* contains his creed ; his poem of *The Ladder of St. Augustine* is the philosophy of his career. Yet I have many times heard him say "the mind cannot be controlled" ; and the fact that he was, when at his best, a poet of inspiration is proved by such poems as *Sandalphon*, *My Lost Youth*, *The Beleaguered City*, *The Fire of Drift Wood*, *Suspiria*, *The Secret of the Sea*, *The Two Angels*, and *The Warden of the Cinque Ports*.

The two writers of whom he oftenest spoke, within my hearing, were Lowell and Hawthorne. Of Lowell he said, "He is one of the manliest and noblest men that ever lived." "Hawthorne often came into this room," he said, "and sometimes he would go there, behind the window curtains, and remain in silent reverie the whole evening. No one disturbed him; he came and went as he liked. He was a mysterious man." With Irving's works he was especially familiar, and he often quoted from them in his talk to me. One summer day at his cottage at Nahant I found him reading Cooper's sea stories, and had the pleasure of hearing from his lips a tribute to that great writer — the foremost novelist in American literature, unmatched since Scott in the power to treat with a free inspiration and vigorous and splendid descriptive skill the vast pageants of nature and to build and sustain ideals of human character worthy of such surroundings. Longfellow was in fine spirits that day, and very happy, and I have always thought of him as he looked then, holding his daughter Edith in his arms — a little child, with long, golden hair, and lovely, merry face — and by his presence making the sunshine brighter and the place more sacred with kindness and peace.

The best portrait of Longfellow is the one

made by Samuel Lawrence ; the best because it gives the noble and spirited poise
and action of his head, shows his clear-cut,
strong, yet delicate features unmasked with
a beard, and preserves that alert, inspired
expression which came into his face when
he was affected by strong emotion. I recall
Mrs. Longfellow's commendation of it, in a
fireside talk. It was her favourite portrait
of him. We discussed Thomas Buchanan
Read's portrait of him, and of his three
daughters, when those pictures were yet
fresh from the easel. I remember speaking
to him of a fancied resemblance between
the face of Mrs. Longfellow and the face of
Evangeline, in Faed's well-known picture.
He said that others had noticed it but that
he did not perceive it. Yet I think those
faces were kindred, in stateliness and in the
mournful beauty of the eyes. It is strange
what trifles crowd upon the memory, when
one thinks of the long ago and the friends
that have departed. I recollect his smile
when he said that he always called to mind
the number of the house in Beacon street,
Boston, — which was Mrs. Longfellow's
home when she was Miss Appleton, — " by
thinking of the Thirty-nine Articles." I
recollect the gentle gravity of his voice when

he showed me a piece of the coffin of Dante, and said, in a low tone, "That has touched his bones." I recollect the benignant look in his eyes and the warm pressure of his hand when he bade me good-bye (it was the last time), saying, "You never forget me — you always come to see me." There were long lapses of time during which I never saw him, being held fast by incessant duties and drifted far away from the moorings of my youth. But as often as I came back to his door his love met me on the threshold and his noble serenity gave me comfort and cheer. It seems but a little while since, in quick and delicate remembrance of the old days, he led me to his hearthstone, saying, "Come and sit in my children's chair." What an awful solemnity, and yet what a soothing sense of perfect nobleness and beneficent love, hallows now that storied home from which his earthly and visible presence has forever departed!

In the summer of 1861, on a day of sunshine and flowers and gently whispering winds, those rooms were hushed and darkened, and a group of mourning friends stood around the sacred relics, beautiful in death, of the poet's wife. Only one voice was heard — the voice of prayer. But every heart prayed for the sufferer, thus awfully stricken and left to bear the burden of a great and endless grief. And then we followed her to the place of her final rest. Here before me is a twig that I broke, that day, from a tree beside her grave. I may keep it now in remembrance of him as well as of her. He fulfilled, within the twenty years following, some of the greatest works of his life; but in all that time he was only waiting for the hour which came to him at last. Through all the grand poise of his being, through his never-ending still beginning labour, through his pensive ways neither mournful nor gay, through his meek but manly acceptance of the events of life, through the high and solemn strains of his later poetry, and through that wistful, haunted look in his venerable, bard-like countenance, this was the one prevailing truth. He was waiting for the end. The world is lonelier for his absence. "Woe is me, that I should gaze upon thy place and find it vacant!"

"O friend! O best of friends! Thy absence more
　　Than the impending night darkens the landscape o'er!"

XIX.

A THOUGHT ON COOPER'S NOVELS.

THE inherent spiritual charms appertaining to different forms of art are not interchangeable. The best Grecians are agreed that something yet remains in Homer that translation has never grasped. The characteristic magic of a romance will not impart its thrill to a drama. Those who, for example, should expect in a play, a reproduction of the soul of Cooper's genius would inevitably be disappointed. Certain dramatic elements his genius and his stories do, indeed, possess ; but the essential quality of them is an evanescent spirit of romance that can no more be cramped within stage-grooves than the notes of a wind-harp can be prisoned in a bird-cage. Often, when Cooper is imaginative, his mind revels over vast spaces, alike in the trackless wilderness and on the trackless ocean — forests that darken half a continent and tremendous icebergs that crash and crumble upon unknown seas. More often he is descriptive and meditative, moralising, like Wordsworth, on rock and river and the tokens of a divine soul in the wonders of creation. His highest mood of feeling is that of calm-eyed philosophy. His highest ideal of virtue is self-sacrifice. His best pictures are too broad in scope and too voluminous in details for illustration to the eye. Neither Jasper's white-winged descent upon the Indian ambuscade, nor the flight of Hutter's ark, nor Chingachgook singing his death-song, nor the mysterious Pilot steering his ship, in night and tempest, through a perilous channel and a thousand dangers of death, could be shown in effigy. His highest figures, moreover, are types of the action that passes within the heart ; of passion that is repressed ; of what is suffered rather than of what is done. He never painted better than when he painted the Pathfinder vanishing on the dusky edge of the forest, after the parting with Mabel ; and in that lovely, pathetic incident, as in many that are kindred with it, there is no particle of dramatic effect. Salient features are alone available for the purpose of the drama, and it is not in salient features that the spell of Cooper's genius resides. The essence of his novels — the wildwood fragrance of fancy and the reiterated yet constantly varied mood of suspense — eludes dramatic treatment. The reader is constantly aware of this charm; never so much aware of it, perhaps, as in that absorbing chapter of the *Mohicans* which describes the beginning of Munro's quest of his daughters, after the massacre. The spectator of a play on the subject would not be aware of it at all. He might be interested, indeed, and at times excited and impressed; but he would no longer be ruled by the massive sincerity of Cooper's feeling and the honest, minute thoroughness of his simple text, and he would be no longer swayed by his own imagination. In the silence of the library the reader may listen with Hawkeye for the rustle of a leaf, or the crackling of a twig, or the lonesome call of the loon across the darkening lake at sunset. In the glare of lamps, and when neither the situation nor the language is ideal, the spectator would perceive his vision limited by the picture before him; the inward ear would close and the inward eye would darken. It is the nature of some books that they lure us into a dream of pleasure and keep us there; and it is the nature of some pictures that they confront fancy with fact and stop our dreaming with a shock. Nothing in Cooper's delineation of wilderness life seems incongruous or absurd to a reader. His books have an atmosphere — like the odour of pine trees on the wind of night — and this the stage could not preserve. They were not written for it and they cannot be fitted to its powers and its needs. They will yield romantic pictures, effective incidents, and various and picturesque characters; but they will not yield their glamour. The poet who brought home the sea-shells found that they had left their beauty on the beach.

XX.

A MAN OF LETTERS: JOHN R. G. HASSARD.

Obiit April 18, 1888.

A PATIENT and noble struggle against inexorable disease has ended, and a friend and comrade — dearer than words can say — has fallen asleep. The duty of recording his death falls naturally upon one who for many years stood nearest his side and was honoured with his affection and confidence. It would, under any circumstances, be a difficult, mournful duty. It is inexpressibly solemn to the friend who writes these words — for not alone is it fitting that love should utter its sense of bereavement, but that thought should express its conviction of public no less than personal loss.

John Hassard was a journalist, but also he was a man of letters, and in both capacities he exerted eminent talents in a conscientious spirit and with passionate loyalty to the highest standard of principle, learn-

ing, and taste.   As a journalist he knew
that the most essential function of the newspaper is the presentation of the news ; but
as a man of letters he was aware that the
pictorial facts and the facts of thought and
feeling are not less actual or less important
than the superficial aspects of the passing
hour.   He treated many subjects, ranging
over a period of many years during which
he was in continuous service of the press
and writing in the different veins of narrative, description, criticism, satire, and des-
ultory comment ; but whatever the subject
he never failed to satisfy his readers that
every material fact had been stated and to
impress their minds with his absolute sincerity, his breadth of view, his wisdom, his
moral principle, his fine taste, and his noble
ideal of social order and personal conduct.
It was that double power, that power of
presenting the picture of actual life and at
the same time of indicating its motive, its
spirit, its accessories and its meaning, that
made him an exceptional force in the profession that he dignified and adorned.

A life that is devoted to the art of writing seems, on its surface, to be uneventful.
There is nothing in it of outward action
and but little of visible deed.   Yet no

greater error could possibly be made, in the study and estimate of human character, than the error of assuming that the life of a true man of letters is necessarily or possibly a life of apathetic monotony and gray stagnation. For such a man lives, not alone under the pressure of his intense individuality, but under the stress and strain of the intellectual movement of his time. Every fresh wave of thought breaks over him. Every aspiration and every forward step of the vanguard mind of his period is to him a personal experience — because he must keep pace with it. The religious question, the political question, the social question, the scientific question — each and every one of these is of vital personal importance to the man of letters. He cannot be content, as so many other people are, merely to hear of those things and to pass them by ; he must think out the problems of the age ; he must reach a conclusion ; he must have convictions ; he must speak his mind. To him is forbidden alike indifference and silence. A moral and mental responsibility rests on him, to serve his generation, to proclaim the truth and defend the right, to help others at the hard part of the way, and thus to fulfil the duty for which he was designed in the drama of human development. There are serious ordeals in the life of such a man — times of sore mental conflict and cruel trial, hours of acute suffering, moments of splendid conquest and joy. Outwardly he seems placid, and the round of his existence looks dull. But under the calm surface of that silver tranquillity the tempests of passion rage and pass, the powers of character are matured and marshalled, and the strife of ideas accomplishes its appointed work. The representative man of letters is not seen in public affairs, and there is but little to tell of him when his career has ended. But his words are in thousands of hearts and his influence lives in a myriad of the good deeds of the men of action who have imperceptibly felt his dominion.

John Hassard's life afforded constant and potent illustration of those views. It was only slightly diversified by events, but it flowed over the depths of a wide, varied, and significant intellectual experience. He was born in New York, in 1836. He was taught and trained in St. John's College at Fordham, from which institution he was graduated in 1855. He assisted in preparing the *New American Encyclopædia* and in 1865 was editor of *The Catholic World.*

In 1865–66 he was a writer for *The Chicago Republican*. He became associated with *The New York Tribune* in 1866, and in various capacities he served that journal for about twenty years. He was an editorial writer, a reviewer, and a musical critic, and for some time after the death of Horace Greeley, in 1872, he held the post of managing editor. He wrote the *Life of Archbishop Hughes* (1866); the *Life of Pope Pius IX.* (1877); a *History of the United States* (1877); *The Ring of the Nibelungs — a Description of its First Performance, in August,* 1876, *at Bayreuth* (1877); and *A Pickwickian Pilgrimage* (1881). He was at Bayreuth in 1876, and his narrative of Wagner's exploits and success at that time — a remarkable epoch in the history of music — is one of fascinating interest, and it is as vital now as when it was written. The sagacity with which he recognised Wagner's power and the precision and authority with which he foreshadowed the drift of that composer's ideas and influence abide among many proofs of his pre-eminent competence and superiority as a musical judge. His *Pickwickian Pilgrimage* was the result of a stroll in England, in the summer of 1879, chiefly in the track of Pick-

wick and his friends. He was an ardent
admirer of the works of Charles Dickens,
and he followed in the footsteps of that
novelist reverently and with affectionate
appreciation. That book contains an account of a boat voyage down the Wye,
from Hereford to Chepstow, which is perhaps the best single example of his best
literary manner that could be chosen — a
manner in which the influence of Goldsmith
and Addison is discernible through the
writer's characteristic mood of keen observation, light, pictorial touch, and gentle
sentiment. Another of his felicitous works
is a pamphlet called *The Fast Printing
Machine* (1878), being a narrative of mechanical dexterity and industrial achievement, but invested with the charm of a
fairy tale and expressed in language of rare
vigour. These few sentences recount the
chief incidents of his life — scarcely more
eventful than that of the Vicar of Wake-
field, with its migration from the brown
bed to the blue and from the blue bed back
again to the brown. It is the old story of
the man of thought, who stands apart from
the pageant of human affairs, moralising
on it as it passes, and striving to purify
and refresh it at the springs.

The actual and essential story of that
life lies deeper and would be found beneath
the surface, in the current of intellectual
development and the analysis of literary
achievement. John Hassard was not one
of the exceptional few who build monuments essentially great in literature and
thus strongly command and permanently
retain the attention and interest of the
world. He was a man of fine talents and
lovely character, who devoted himself to
the service of journalism, and who made
his mark in that field — broad, strong, brilliant, and noble. The great public of mis-
cellaneous readers cannot rationally be
supposed to cherish a deep interest in such
a personality for a great length of time after
its career has ended. But it was a personality that blessed many who never heard of
it, while those whose privilege it was to
know his labours and their value will ten-
derly meditate now upon the beautiful traits
of his mind, the charm of his companionship, and the lesson of his pure, blameless,
devoted, beneficent life. He would have
been the first to reprove extravagant eulogy
of his talents or his productions. He filled
a difficult and delicate office with rare ability and discretion. He taught, by example,

the primal necessity of being perfectly well
acquainted with the art he discussed.   He
studied constantly, he thought deeply, he
worked conscientiously and with laborious
zeal.   His freedom from conventionality
and prejudice was a continual monition of
refreshing originality of view and justice of
mood.   He looked at every subject with
present eyes, not with the eyes of the past.
The word that he spoke was the word of
to-day, not of yesterday, and he never fell
into the error of mistaking his personal
distaste for a defect in the artist or the
work reviewed.   He knew, with Coleridge,
that the first requisite for a good critic is
a good heart, and he proved that he knew
it, every time he took up his pen.   His keen
intuition as to the relative importance of
persons and themes was constantly manifested and was still another lesson of practical value.   For this journalist and man of
letters, this devotee of art and music — who
often sat alone for hours playing upon the
organ the music that he loved, — was also
a man of the world.   He possessed the
sense of proportion and fitness, an old-time
courtliness of thinking as well as of manner, a sense of the right place for trifles,
and a happy faculty for silence.   He was

not envious and he was not meddlesome.
He never thought it to be his duty to regu-
late the musical criticism of the general
press. If he wanted a good criticism of an
opera to be printed he endeavoured to write
it himself, instead of writing querulous
observations condemnatory of the remarks
of contemporary journals. It was another
of his admirable and exemplary qualities
that he perceived the critical duty of giving
encouragement. He looked into the future
of the artist, and he could be wisely len-
ient. In the fulfilment of his duty he
thought of himself last, or not at all, while
his dignity was of the natural kind that is
always present. Education and experience
taught him how to use fine faculties for the
best advantage of others.

Among the old-fashioned phrases of
eulogy there is one that long usage has
rendered conventional; but it is very expressive: He was a gentleman and a
scholar. It is much to deserve those names.
John Hassard entirely deserved them, and
he bore them with the sweet modesty,
unconscious humility, and native and winning gentleness of an unselfish nature. He
was always thoughtful for others; always
doing acts of courtesy and kindness. He

was ever to be found on the side of chivalry
toward women, and his active considera-
tion for young people, especially for working boys, and his sweet manner toward
children much endeared him wherever he
went. His reading was large and various.
He was accomplished in the classics; he
had comprehensive knowledge of English
literature; and he possessed both the
French language and the German. As a
reviewer he early acquired the excellent
method, so long pursued and with such
good result by the late George Ripley —
the father of the art in America. That
method was to assume the author's point of
view; to let the book declare itself, its contents, its style, character, and intention;
and then to discuss it as a literary artist, an
observer, a thinker, and from essential
environments of its subject. He was
rarely severe and never unkind. He could
condemn explicitly, but he stated the
grounds of his judgment, and they were
invariably logical and sound. He was
remarkably expert in perceiving the beauties of art, and he loved to praise; and,
as he knew what had been done by others
and was quick to see the fresh touch and
understand the subtle suggestion, his praise

gave pleasure, rewarded merit, encouraged high endeavour, and was valuable. His sympathies went with the imagination and the affections, in literature, not with the morbid passions and not with the "realistic" movement in any of its phases. He rightly abhorred the art represented by M. Zola; he justly despised the whole brood of Ouida novelists; and, in common with other sane persons, he smiled at the weakness, which, mistaking the assertion of power for power itself, accepts such writings as those of the late Walt Whitman for poetry. He was sufficiently conservative to love the novels of Scott and the poems of Crabbe, and he was sufficiently comprehensive, acute, and fair-minded, while recognising the passion and splendour of Byron, to appreciate and exult in the philosophic grandeur, the solemn tenderness, the beautiful simplicity, and the comforting faith of Wordsworth. Those are significant indications of the character of his mind, the mood in which he lived and laboured, and the ideals toward which he strove.

And so he passed into his rest. He was a bright and gentle presence in the life of every man and woman to whom he was ever known. He lived a good life. He suffered patiently. He met his fate with humble resignation and firm composure. He helped, in a material degree, to advance the standard of musical art and literary taste in the republic. He has left critical essays which are models of searching thought, just judgment, cheering sympathy, and felicitous expression. The sketches with which he enriched our literature in its lighter branches are of singular beauty, graceful in their form and movement, often illumined with playful humour, always vital with the appreciative sincerity of critical enthusiasm. His biographical writings are discriminative, judicious, and truthful, and are couched in a terse and lucid style. He was a devout man, rigid in his principles and pure in his life; but he was invariably charitable, magnanimous, and tender in his judgment of others. No human being was ever more quick than he to appreciate merit or to forgive frailty and palliate defect. He was much beloved; he is deeply mourned; and he will long be remembered.

THE END.

WANDERERS;

BEING

A Collection of the Poems of William Winter.

New Edition, Revised and Enlarged. With
a Portrait of the Author.

18MO, CLOTH, 75 CENTS.

Also a Limited LARGE PAPER EDITION, printed
on English Hand-made Paper. Price $2.50.

"But it has seemed to the author of these poems—
which of course are offered as absolutely impersonal
—that they are the expression of various representative
moods of human feeling and various representative
aspects of human experience, and that therefore they
may possibly possess the inherent right to exist."—
From the Preface.

"The verse of Mr. Winter is dedicated mainly to
love and wine, to flowers and birds and dreams, to the
hackneyed and never-to-be-exhausted repertory of the
old singers. His instincts are strongly conservative; his
confessed aim is to belong to 'that old school of English
Lyrical Poetry, of which gentleness is the soul, and
simplicity the garment.'"— *Saturday Review.*

"The poems have a singular charm in their graceful
spontaneity."— *Scots Observer.*

"Free from cant and rant—clear cut as a cameo,
pellucid as a mountain brook. It may be derided as
trite, *borné*, unimpassioned; but in its own modest
sphere it is, to our thinking, extraordinarily successful,
and satisfies us far more than the pretentious mouthing
which receives the seal of over-hasty approbation."—
Athenæum.

MACMILLAN & CO.,

66 FIFTH AVENUE,   NEW YORK.

SHADOWS OF THE STAGE.

18MO, CLOTH, 75 CENTS.

"The fame of the actor more than that of any other artist is an evanescent one — a 'bubble reputation' — indeed, and necessarily so from the conditions under which his genius is exercised. While the impression it makes is often more vivid and inspiring for the moment than that of the poet and the painter, it vanishes almost with the occasion which gave it birth, and lives only as a tradition in the memory of those to whom it had immediately appealed. 'Shadows they are, and shadows they pursue.'

"The writer, therefore, who, gifted with insight and a poetic enthusiasm which enables him to discern on the one hand the beauties in a dramatic work not perceived by the many, and on the other the qualities in the actor which have made him a true interpreter of the poet's thought, at the same time possessing the faculty of revealing to us felicitously the one, and the other is certainly entitled to our grateful recognition.

"Such a writer is Mr. William Winter, easily the first, — for we know of none other living in this country, or in the England he loves so much, in whose nature the critic's vision is united with that of the poet so harmoniously. . . .

"Over and above all this, there is in these writings the same charm of style, poetic glamour and flavor of personality which distinguish whatever comes to us from Mr. Winter's pen, and which make them unique in our literature." — *Home Journal*, New York.

MACMILLAN & CO.,

66 FIFTH AVENUE, NEW YORK.

OLD SHRINES AND IVY.

18MO, CLOTH, 75 CENTS.

CONTENTS.

SHRINES OF HISTORY.

SHRINES OF LITERATURE.

"Whatever William Winter writes is marked by felicity of diction and by refinement of style, as well as by the evidence of culture and wide reading. 'Old Shrines and Ivy' is an excellent example of the charm of his work."— *Boston Courier*.

MACMILLAN & CO.,

66 FIFTH AVENUE, NEW YORK.

SHAKESPEARE'S

ENGLAND.

18MO, CLOTH, 75 CENTS.

" . . . It was the author's wish, in dwelling thus upon the rural loveliness, and the literary and historical associations of that delightful realm, to afford sympathetic guidance and useful suggestion to other American travellers who, like himself, might be attracted to roam among the shrines of the mother-land. Temperament is the explanation of style; and he has written thus of England because she has filled his mind with beauty and his heart with mingled joy and sadness; and surely some memory of her venerable ruins, her ancient shrines, her rustic glens, her gleaming rivers, and her flower-spangled meadows will mingle with the last thoughts that glimmer through his brain when the shadows of the eternal night are falling and the ramble of life is done." — *From the Preface.*

"He offers something more than guidance to the American traveller. He is a convincing and eloquent interpreter of the august memories and venerable sanctities of the old country." — *Saturday Review.*

"The book is delightful reading." — *Scribner's Monthly.*

"Enthusiastic and yet keenly critical notes and comments on English life and scenery." — *Scotsman.*

MACMILLAN & CO.,

66 FIFTH AVENUE, NEW YORK.

GRAY DAYS
AND GOLD.

18MO, CLOTH, 75 CENTS.

CONTENTS.

Classic Shrines.
        Haunted Glens and Houses.
The Haunts of Moore.   Old York.
      Beautiful Bath.
          The Lakes and Fells of Wordsworth.
Shakespeare Relics at Worcester.
    Byron and Hucknall Torkard.
        Historic Nooks and Corners.
Up and Down the Avon.   Shakespeare's Town.
    Rambles in Arden.
       The Stratford Fountain.
         Bosworth Field.
           The Home of Dr. Johnson.
From London to Edinburgh.
    Into the Highlands.
        Highland Beauties.
           The Heart of Scotland.
Elegiac Memorials.   Sir Walter Scott.
    Scottish Pictures.
       Imperial Ruins.
          The Land of Marmion.
            At Vesper Time.

This book, which is intended as a companion to
Shakespeare's England, relates to the gray days of an
American wanderer in the British Isles, and to the gold
of thought and fancy that can be found there.

MACMILLAN & CO.,

66 FIFTH AVENUE,   NEW YORK.

GRAY DAYS
AND GOLD.

18MO, CLOTH, 75 CENTS.

PRESS NOTICES.

"Mr. Winter's graceful and meditative style in his English sketches has recommended his earlier volume upon (Shakespeare's) England to many readers, who will not need urging to make the acquaintance of this companion book, in which the traveller guides us through the quiet and romantic scenery of the mother-country with a mingled affection and sentiment of which we have had no example since Irving's day." — *The Nation.*

"As friendly and good-humoured a book on English scenes as any American has written since Washington Irving." — *Daily News, London.*

"Much that is bright and best in our literature is brought once more to our dulled memories. Indeed, we know of but few volumes containing so much of observation, kindly comment, philosophy, and artistic weight as this unpretentious little book." — *Chicago Herald.*

"They who have never visited the scenes which Mr. Winter so charmingly describes will be eager to do so in order to realize his fine descriptions of them, and they who have already visited them will be incited by his eloquent recital of their attractions to repeat their former pleasant experiences." — *Public Ledger, Philadelphia.*

MACMILLAN & CO.,

66 FIFTH AVENUE,   NEW YORK.